Graced by Pines

The Ponderosa Pine in the American West

Alexandra Murphy

Illustrated by Robert Petty

MOUNTAIN PRESS PUBLISHING COMPANY
MISSOULA, MONTANA 1994

Part of the poem "Foxtail Pine" by Gary Snyder (page 12) is reprinted from *The Backcountry* by Gary Snyder, by permission of New Directions Publishing Corp. Copyright © 1983 by Gary Snyder.

Tewa Pueblo prayer (page 33) is reprinted from *People of Chaco: A Canyon and Its Culture* by Kendrick Frazier, by permission of W. W. Norton & Company, Inc. Copyright © 1986 by Kendrick Frazier.

The coyote story (pages 46–47) is reprinted from "The Ram's Horn Tree and Other Medicine Trees of the Flathead Indians" by George F. Weisel, Jr. *The Montana Magazine of History* (July 1951) 1:5–13. Reprinted by permission of George F. Weisel, Jr.

Library of Congress Cataloging-in-Publication Data

Murphy, Alexandra, 1963–
    Graced by pines : the Ponderosa pine in the American West / Alexandra Murphy ; illustrated by Robert Petty.
        p. cm.
    Includes bibliographical references (p.   ).
    ISBN 0-87842-307-9 : $10.00
    1. Ponderosa pine—West (U.S.) 2. Ponderosa pine—West (U.S.)—Folk-lore. I. Title.
QK494.5.P66M87 1994
585' .2—dc20   94-29803
                                                                                     CIP

Printed in U.S.A. on recycled paper.
Mountain Press Publishing Company
P. O. Box 2399 • Missoula, Montana 59801
(406) 728-1900

For Robert

Contents

Acknowledgments

I would like to thank William Kittredge, David Pepi, and Paul Dietrich for their support and advice during the formative stages of this book. My deep gratitude to Deborah Richie, for guidance, faith, and encouragement. To Duane Duff, Stephen Arno, Adella Begaye, Lucy Vanderburg, and James Habeck for reviewing sections of the manuscript for accuracy. And to my husband, Robert, whose love and wisdom have so fully graced these explorations.

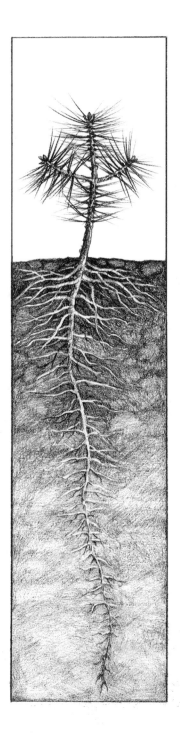

Introduction

I have come from Missoula, driving an hour west on Route 90, to see the largest ponderosa pine in Montana. Up a dirt road along Fish Creek, I turn onto a track that circles within a few hundred feet of the tree. I can see it from my car and am instantly disappointed—it looks big, but not nearly as massive as I had imagined.

Walking closer, I see the deception of distance. The old pine is immense. When I wrap my arms around it, they stretch out nearly straight from my sides. At last measuring, the tree was six and one-half feet in diameter—twenty feet in circumference. Its bark is smoother and lighter than any I have seen, the ground beneath it washed with golden flakes of bark.

The pine stretches 194 feet above me, fifteen stories high and still growing. Cicero said that when you enter a tall grove of trees, you experience the presence of a deity. After decades of clear-cutting along Fish Creek, this tree is no longer part of a tall grove, but running my fingers over the curves and furrows of its bark, I am like a blind man reading holy text. I stand on sacred ground.

Reverence for trees and for pines in particular roots deep in human history. Greek mythology celebrates the story of Pitys, a nymph who was the lover of Boreas, god of the North Wind. Pitys fell in love with the wild wood god, Pan, and when Boreas discovered this, he hurled Pitys against a rock in rage. She instantly transformed into a pine, her roots clinging to the rock, her blood and tears of grief becoming droplets of golden resin that oozed from her wounded limbs.

To the ancient Phrygians, pine cones were symbols of fertility, and they offered cones at the sacred vaults of the earth goddess, Demeter, to ensure a bountiful harvest and many children. Romans honored the fiery goddess Cybele on the vernal equinox by processing to her temple with a pine tree draped in clothing and decorated with violets. Worshipers lashed themselves and sprinkled their blood on the pine, in hopes that they might share in Cybele's passion. In Japanese tradition, the pine represents longevity and balance. And during the darkest time of the year, lit with candles or bulbs, pines celebrate the advent of hope—of longer days, new life, the turning of another season.

Every cohesive culture has myths by which its members live, stories that teach the people who they are, how they fit into the natural order, and how to live sustainably on the earth. Before European settlement began, more than nine million people inhabited North America, members of hundreds of distinct tribes. The communal stories of these tribes formed the weft of their social fabric—their knowledge of community history, moral code, and survival skills. The natural world was the warp upon which these stories found their form and meaning. In many Native American traditions, each story calls to mind a specific part of the landscape, and, in turn, each part of the landscape calls to mind a story. When asked about the importance of a particular spring that was the setting of a tribal story, a Pueblo elder replied, "It's good we have that water. We need it to live. It's good we have that spring. We need it to live right." Through these stories, the American landscape, in all its vast wildness, became intimately known and celebrated.

When European settlers began killing Native Americans— slaughtering whole communities, decimating and disbanding others— they forfeited the stories that had illuminated the land. Without story to explain the natural world and express its value, history, and beauty, the conquering Europeans experienced America as a truly hostile wilderness—alien, immense, amoral, and terrifying. And thus vulnerable to destruction. "When nothing is sacred, nothing is safe," John Hay wrote. Our rapacious relationship with the American landscape bears this out.

Western America is still only sparsely reinvested with story. During its brief history of European settlement, it has been largely populated by explorers and exploiters who have used each place while its fortunes lasted, then moved on, leaving behind scarred and depleted land and taking with them their stories and experience and knowledge of that place. Just as soil without roots is vulnerable to erosion, so the West has suffered from the rootlessness of its human inhabitants. Its cities and towns and wild lands still lack the communal memory that renders a place valuable and sacred to humans. "No place," wrote Wallace Stegner, "is a place until things that have happened in it are remembered in history, ballads, yarns, legends, or monuments." Such remembrance requires stability and continuity and love of place that come from a long association akin to marriage.

In the cultural void that transience and placelessness create, mistaken mythologies have emerged—belief in limitless abundance and open space, that rain will follow the plow, that technology will overcome any problems we create or encounter in the land, that the West can simply be an extension of the East if we manipulate it enough.

Such early visionaries as John Wesley Powell warned that this myopia would damage the land and ultimately fail us, but it is only now, when our frontiers are filled and we have nowhere else to go, that we are seeing the West as if for the first time. And when we look, we see that the wide-open spaces are partitioned with barbed-wire fence rows and subdivisions. The animals we associate most with the mythic West—bison, grizzly bears, bighorn sheep, wolves, and mountain lions—roam isolated pockets of their historic ranges.

3

Rivers flow dirty and dammed, rangelands turn dusty and cactus-covered, brown air shrouds sprawling towns and cities.

Like a coyote hollowing a bed in sand, the work of restorying the West is a steady turning in place by which we will lay spiritual claim to the land and find ourselves, finally, at home. Just as Thoreau mythologized Walden Pond by digging deep into its essence and uncovering its history, its rhythms, its idiosyncrasies, and its beauty, so we must learn and share the stories of the West. Many writers, musicians, and artists have begun this work; much more remains to be done.

Donald Culross Peattie wrote, "If you know your West at all, you know its Yellow [ponderosa] Pine." These pines grow in every state west of the Great Plains, from Kansas to California, from North Dakota to Texas. In the Southwest, they grow at elevations over nine thousand feet; on the Oregon coast, near sea level. They root in almost any soil, from gravelly glacial till and volcanic ash in the Pacific Northwest to loose sands in the Southwest deserts. They can survive on less than twelve inches of rain a year in places where the ground surface temperatures exceed 160 degrees Fahrenheit in midsummer.

The stories of this narrative are drawn from my experiences in ponderosa pine country—eight years of living in southern Utah and two years in Missoula, Montana, and from travels through pine forests in Oregon, California, Arizona, New Mexico, Colorado, and Texas. The people who have helped reveal these stories are those who know the pine in some way—craftspeople, mill workers, activists, ecologists, botanists, foresters, nature writers, and ponderosa pine admirers.

Pines are living constants in the landscape. They hold the West's history, both in the rings of their heartwood, hidden within like human memory, and in the outward manifestations of their daily living—in their blackened fire scars, the borings of beetles and woodpeckers, the goshawk nests high in their wolfy crowns, the wind-sculpted drape of their branches, and the stumps, smooth as tables, left by logging. By apprehending this history, we come to know the pines, and in turn, to know the West.

Like the rest of the American landscape, ponderosa pine stands have changed substantially since white settlement began. Though most field guides still refer to these pines as growing in open, parklike stands, few such stands remain. For more than a century, logging and fire suppression have changed the face and heart of ponderosa pine forests in the West. Trees four feet in diameter and two hundred feet tall were once commonplace. Now they are the exception in forests crowded with young pines and Douglas-firs.

At a time when we are so rapidly transforming the West's forests, we are only beginning to fathom the effects of these changes—the extent to which the loss of ancient ponderosa pine forests reflects a physical and spiritual depletion in the landscape and in ourselves. In pygmy legend, there was once a young boy who found a bird with a beautiful song in the forest and brought it home. His father refused to spare food for a mere bird and killed it instead. As he did so, the father dropped dead. By killing the bird, he killed its song, and by killing the song, he killed himself. It is with this story in mind that I relate what I have heard of the ponderosa pine's wild song.

Robert Petty

1

A Tree Called Ponderosa

In 1803 President Thomas Jefferson commissioned his personal secretary, Captain Meriwether Lewis, to explore the wilds of the northwest region of what is now the United States. Lewis, then twenty-nine years old, accepted readily and chose for his co-leader thirty-three-year-old retired captain William Clark. Jefferson instructed the men to find the fabled Northwest Passage, a waterway that could link the Pacific and Atlantic Oceans with minimal overland travel. In the process, their explorations would reinforce American claims to Oregon country, then eyed covetously by the British.

Jefferson wanted to know as much as he could about this virtually unexplored territory. He sent Lewis to school in Philadelphia to study botany, zoology, and celestial navigation, and asked the men to record in detail the landscape, the people, and the plants and animals they encountered.

In those northwest lands were thousands of plants and animals—dazzling birds, large mammals, magnificent trees—and whole mountain ranges, rivers, and valleys unknown to eastern scientists in a land so unlike the East as to belie continuity with it. Landscapes painted by a mad artist, with broad, angular strokes, bold hues, impossible depths and distances. An explorer's paradise.

Lewis and Clark embarked on their journey from St. Louis with seven tons of food, 175 pounds of gunpowder, thirty gallons of brandy, eighteen journals bound in red morocco leather, and the presidential mantle of authority to name all they saw.

The arrogance of bestowing and assuming such authority was both predictable and profound. For the hundreds of thousands of Native Americans living in what would become the western United States, the land was already fully, richly named. The pine tree that Lewis first recorded near Orofino, Idaho, and named "long-leaf pine" already had many tribal names. To the Navajo, it was 'ndísh chíí, meaning "red pine." The Cheyenne knew the pine as séstotóe and its cone as heskóve-vovotse, meaning "thorny egg." To the Crow, it was báachiia, to the Salish, caqʷljʹ. Lewis's chosen name seems decidedly dull by comparison.

The expedition cut logs from this pine to make dugout canoes for their trip down the Clearwater River. Lewis collected a specimen, as he did with many of the plants and animals he discovered, so that it could be officially documented when he returned to Washington. Few specimens survived the long expedition, however, without decomposing. And in 1809, riding back to Washington, D.C., Lewis died of gunshot wounds along the Natchez Trace in the wilds of Tennessee. Some claimed it was murder, but Jefferson and others who were familiar with Lewis's bouts of depression suspected suicide. In the confusion following his death, Lewis's personal field notes were lost and the pine forgotten.

Twenty-five years later, Scottish botanist David Douglas rediscovered the pine near Spokane, Washington, and officially named it *Pinus ponderosa*, a name whose depth seems more worthy of the tree. Lewis's name celebrated a single physical feature of the pine, but Douglas's name suggests the tree's character, its spirit as well as its physical nature. *Ponderosa* comes from the Latin *ponderosus*, meaning "heavy, weighty, significant." Its root, *pondus*, means "weight of words or thoughts, influence, equilibrium, constancy." The verb form, *pondero*, means "to mentally weigh, to reflect upon."

A walk through a grove of mature ponderosa pines reveals the aptness of this title. In his notes, Douglas remarked that the pines often exceeded "four feet in diameter, three feet above the ground, carrying their thickness to a very great height, frequently measuring eighteen inches in diameter at seventy feet." Though he devoted little space in his journals to unscientific reverie, Douglas jotted the pine's praises, calling it "very elegant" and "highly ornamental," grand compliments for a man sparing in his words.

The name's allusion to the significance and influence of the pine is borne out in the pine's role in western human and natural history. Evidence of human use of ponderosa pines dates to A.D. 900. In Chaco Canyon, Pueblo Anasazi used more than 150,000 ponderosa pine logs to build such architectural masterpieces as Chetro Ketl and Pueblo Bonito. Ponderosa pines provided the lumber that built western boom towns from Custer to Spokane, from Helena to Cedar City. They formed the rail ties that connected them, and the mining timbers that, at least temporarily, braced their economies.

Hundreds of species of animals depend in part or whole on the pine for their livelihood. The tassel-eared squirrel, found only in ponderosa pine forests of the Southwest, depends entirely on the pine for food and shelter. Scores of other animals eat its seeds, burrow in its bark, nest in its branches, excavate its heartwood, and browse the grasses that grow in its sun-dappled shade.

The tree embodies, too, the qualities of equilibrium and constancy. Ponderosa pines live today that were well established on their sunny slopes five centuries ago. Naturalist Enos Mills counted 1,047 growth rings in the trunk of a healthy ponderosa pine felled by loggers in Arizona.

The name ponderosa will evoke similar images among people who have seen it. Like a box, the name gathers and contains a kaleidoscope of images—memories of its sweet fragrance, its bark chips as varied as snowflakes, its shining needles. Even for those who have never seen the tree, its name has become synonymous with the mythic Wild West. A generation of Americans grew up watching scenes from Ben Cartwright's high desert ranch, The Ponderosa, on the television show *Bonanza*. For them, the name calls to mind a common vision of the western landscape—wide, fenceless expanses of short-grass plains outlined by white-capped Sierra peaks, a Stetsoned cowhand spurring his horse across a tree-lined horizon. Motels and restaurants a thousand miles from the nearest pine grove borrow its name, lending a touch of wildness to tame facades.

In the years since Douglas first gave the pine its Latin title, botanists have named it even more precisely, identifying three distinct subspecies. Subspecies usually differ from one another in some consistent, morphological or genetic way, but sometimes their distinction is purely geographic. *Pinus ponderosa ponderosa* grows mainly in California's Sierras and in Oregon and Washington. *Pinus ponderosa scopulorum* grows in the Rocky Mountains and southwest regions. The mature pines of both varieties have flaky, golden bark, three- to five-inch mahogany cones, and needles generally grouped in bunches of three. The *scopulorum* variety has a generally smaller stature than the other subspecies, though this may be due as much to growing conditions as to genetic variations.

The third subspecies is markedly different. *Pinus ponderosa arizonica*, better known as Arizona pine, grows mainly in the mountains of Mexico, but ranges into the Chiricahua, Santa Catalina, and Animas Mountains of southeast Arizona and southwest New Mexico. Though it has the same luminous bark as the other two, its needles grow in bundles of five and its cones are only two to three inches long.

To most westerners, the tree in all its variations is simply yellow pine, a name drawn from the color of the mature pine's bark. But bark color is the pine's most changeable trait and has earned it more names than any other. The bark of young pines is black and lusterless. As the pine grows, the bark gradually lightens until, usually at an age of 125 to 150 years, it turns a luminous gold. This transformation has yielded such names as Montana black pine, Sierra brownbark pine, and western red pine. Foresters generally distinguish two forms of the tree, referring to young pines as blackjacks and mature pines as yellow pines. Ponderosa pines continue to grow long after their bark lightens to gold. They can reach diameters of four, five, and six or more feet. Pine admirers call these giants yellowbellies.

John Muir, intimately familiar with the tree's nuances, called the ponderosa "Silver pine." The distinguished title likely stems from his experience of gazing up at the long, waxy needles on a bright, windy day. He wrote:

> [I]t is during cloudless wind-storms that these colossal Pines are most impressively beautiful. They bow like Willows, their leaves streaming forward all in one direction, and, when the sun shines upon them at the required angle, entire groves glow as if every leaf were burnished silver.

No single name, however thoughtfully rendered, can ultimately define the ponderosa pine or any other thing. A name contains the named as banks contain a river. A river can move beyond the confines of its banks, and it is here that discovery begins. I live in southern Utah, a stone's throw from the Escalante River. Most of the year, the Escalante is a placid brook compared to greater western rivers—the Colorado, the Missouri, the Columbia. For most of the year, it runs clear and hunches low between sandy banks, a narrow, gleaming ribbon between monolithic sandstone walls. Where I live, at its confluence with Calf Creek, you can cross its ten-foot width with dry knees, most days.

Given the right conditions, though—deep snowpack on the Aquarius Plateau, a hot spell in early May, a good rainfall or two—the Escalante becomes a foaming, crashing giant. Runoff from a hundred square miles hurls sand, boulders, and logs into the drainage. The river rises in a matter of minutes, swallowing its banks, engulfing dry ground. The canyon floor is two hundred feet wide below my house. There are those who say they have seen the river fill it from wall to wall. Grass and twigs caught in the crooks of cottonwood branches six feet above the normal waterline show the truths of their tales.

Just as a river is sure to overflow and redefine its banks, so the named will outgrow and reshape its name. One seeks the banks to find the river, to have a solid point of departure. But knowing the banks is not knowing the river—the name does not confer full knowledge. Gary Snyder writes:

> Bark smells like pineapple: Jeffries
> cones prick your hand: Ponderosa
>
> Nobody knows what they are, saying
> "needles three to a bunch . . ."

The pine called ponderosa does carry needles three to a bunch. But in the brown-needled humus of its forests, I have also seen bunches of two, four, and five. Though its trunk is yellow, I find in its bark hints of orange, burgundy, rust, and bronze. In the heart of the gold-columned forest, all names and measures fall away like gossamer, and there are only the pines.

2

Climbing

GETTING TO KNOW THE PONDEROSA PINE demands taking risks. To know a pine, you need to meet it where it lives, take off your gloves and feel its bark, roll in its needles, taste its seeds, listen to its music. You need to visit it in all kinds of weather, to observe its moods in sun and rain, on windy days and calm. And so I set out one warm, late-winter day up Rattlesnake Creek near Missoula, Montana, to climb a pine.

Climbing a pine was a risky proposition because I don't consider myself much of a tree climber or a climber of any sort. As a child, I'd hoist myself into the weeping willow that drooped over our pond, push off one well-worn branch, and swing from a long rope that hung from its highest branch. I'd climb the red pines by our house and swing by my knees from their scratchy branches. But now I feel an acid twinge in my belly as I peer over a cliffedge or scramble up a steep slickrock slope, intimidated by gravity, chastened by mortality.

But I went to the Rattlesnake to know the ponderosa pine in a new way. I wanted to see the pine as Muir had seen it when he climbed one in the Sierras during a windstorm, its great trunk swaying like wheatgrass while Muir rode high in its branches. For most of my life, I have viewed the world from the ground up and seen only the undersides of pine branches. I wanted to see them as the barred owl sees them when it perches in twilight on a topmost branch. I wanted to ride the waves of wind on a living raft, to see up close the play of light on tousled needles. And I wanted to hear the ponderosa pine's music from a seat within the tree itself. Muir wrote, "If you would catch the tones of separate needles, climb a tree."

I first became acquainted with the pine on the high plateaus of southern Utah. There, as in much of the West, ponderosa pines grow in pure stands, with few other tree species for hundreds of acres until the terrain dips down, inviting piñon and juniper, or a spring rises to the surface, coaxing water-loving aspen from the soil.

The plateaus of Zion and Bryce Canyon National Parks have some of the finest ponderosa pine forests in Utah, forests that have not been logged in decades, some that have never been cut. Widely spaced columns hold lacy crowns high overhead. Sunlight filters through their latticework and pools on a soft, gold mat of fallen needles. Iridescent wildflowers and evergreen groundcovers—shooting stars and fairy slippers, kinnikinnick, Oregon

grape, and manzanita— thrive in the tannin-rich soil. On these remote plateaus are the open, parklike stands once so typical of the ponderosa pine community.

But ponderosa pine stands are not parklike in the human-made, manicured sense. A healthy ponderosa pine forest has dead snags pitted with pileated woodpecker excavations and fallen logs riddled with beetles and fungi. The living trees are often bowed and scarred, with bulbous knobs and burls or deep, twisted scars from fire and lightning.

On cloudless July days in southern Utah—when every animal with any sense is motionless until dusk, and I can lie like a fish in a deep, smooth pothole in Calf Creek and get hot and dusty again in the few steps back to the house—I drive to nearby Boulder Mountain, over eleven thousand feet high, and walk among ponderosa pines. Winter comes to the mountain in early November and leaves grudgingly in June. July is spring there, and both meadows and forests explode in color.

Highway 12 winds across the south shoulder of the mountain and cuts through wide, bunchgrass meadows and pure stands of spindly aspens. Where wet gully meets warm, southern slopes, aspens intermix with ponderosa pines—smooth, pale green trunks mingle with rough, amber bark; translucent, heart-shaped leaves brush waxy needles. In a few places, Engelmann spruces lend green-black sprays of stubby needles and steel-gray bark to the portrait. Lupines, columbines, and penstemons splash periwinkle, lemon, and lavender across the foreground. A vista of the redrock Waterpocket Fold, the snow-capped Henry Mountains, the angular ridge of the Circle Cliffs and the Kaiparowits Plateau, and the smooth dome of Navajo Mountain forms the backdrop. The exuberant hand of creation slaps its brush with abandon here.

On dryer, southern slopes, ponderosa pines grow alone, and it is here I like best to walk. I can smell the pines even before I see them; their fresh, clear scent fills the grove. When friends plan to visit our home, I tell them to stop on their way over Boulder Mountain and smell a ponderosa pine. Climb out of the car, I say, amble over to one of those grand, roadside pines, press your nose deep into a resinous fissure and breathe deep. In that fragrance lies the essence of this land.

Some days the pines smell like vanilla, other days like butterscotch. Sometimes they hardly smell at all. Their scent comes from volatile oils, called terpenes, in the pines' resin. Because the amount of terpenes released increases as the resin heats up, the trees smell strongest on a warm, sunny day.

The ponderosa pine forests on Boulder Mountain are by no means pristine. These pines were the highest-value, lowest-elevation trees on the plateau, so they were the first to be cut when logging began in earnest a century ago. Still, some of the pine stands were only partially cut, and beautiful three- and four-foot-wide, gold-columned pines remain, reaching high above the second-growth trees around them.

When I say their trunks are golden, I speak in generalities, for their bark is as rich and varied as an impressionist painting. In Van Gogh's painting *The Sower*, the overall sense of the field, when

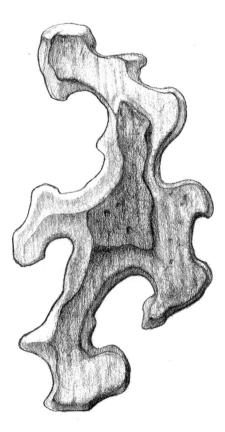

viewed from a distance, is golden. Look closely, though, and brush strokes of pale green, rust, violet, and indigo appear. As a ponderosa pine matures, its bark becomes more and more scaly, sloughing off in thin, irregular shapes that fit together like pieces of a jigsaw puzzle. Every piece is a fine sculpture, with delicate curves and smoothly angled edges like beveled glass. Close up, each scale reflects its own palette of color, from pale yellow to burgundy to black. Step back several feet and the bark pieces blend into a golden masterpiece.

It was such a masterpiece as this that I used for my late-winter climb—my favorite ponderosa pine in the Rattlesnake area. In truth, it's my favorite meadow pine there, and meadow pines are far easier to climb than forest ones. Although mature, forest-grown ponderosa pines are enticingly wide-trunked and have thick sprays of branches at their crowns, they usually lack limbs along the lower stretch of their trunks, often for as much as fifty feet. Ponderosa pines thrive in the sun and perish in the shade, and their branches do the same. The lower branches of a forest-grown pine receive too little light to photosynthesize effectively, so they die and eventually break off.

The pine I chose to climb is odd in some ways, not as picture-perfect as the ponderosas in most guidebooks. Its main stem died during the tree's early years, and four side branches had risen to compete for the lead. None—or perhaps all—had won, so the tree had grown with four main trunks for, judging from its three-foot-thick base, at least 150 years. Some loggers call trees like this "school marms," a name scorning both single teachers and asym-metrical trees, since such trees render less useful lumber than single-trunked trees and so are considered unproductive.

The surplus of main trunks suited me fine, since it would give me more surface area to grasp, and I climbed easily through the first several feet. As I pulled myself up through the branches, flaking bark chips dropped into my mouth, eyes, and hair like confetti. In spite of this, ponderosa pines make ideal climbing trees, since their branches are neither too closely bunched nor too far apart and are stout enough to support a person's weight. Both the larch and the Douglas-fir, two conifers that commonly grow alongside the ponderosa pine in western Montana, have closely spaced, spindly branches that make climbing a difficult, prickly experience.

Even growing in a bright, open meadow, this pine had dead branches interspersed with live ones, and I stepped on the dead ones tentatively as I made my way up the tree. One dead branch had broken away from the trunk, but still hung in the tree, caught among other branches. Foresters call these dangling limbs "widow makers," since a gust of wind can send them hurtling to the ground like a sledgehammer.

Climbing higher, I came eye-level with a cluster of matted, misshapen branches. Their twig ends curled back on themselves, and their needles bristled in a thick profusion, like porcupine quills. Various fungi can cause such a deformation, called a witch's broom, but these branches were covered with the rubbery, yellow stems of dwarf mistletoe. Though it bears little resemblance to the mistletoe of Christmas-kisses fame, dwarf mistletoe is similarly parasitic, its roots drawing sugar from the pine's inner bark.

In mild infestations like this one, dwarf mistletoe simply deforms the pine and reduces its growth rate. Severe infestations can kill a pine and infect entire groves. A spectacular method of reproduction spreads dwarf mistletoe seeds through the pine forest. As a mistletoe seed matures on the female plant, the stalk on which it grows bends lower and lower. When the seed is fully ripe, the skin surrounding it contracts quickly, and the seed bursts into the air like a rock from a slingshot. It can travel as fast as sixty miles per hour, with enough force to carry it thirty feet from the parent plant. The sticky, barbed seed, if successful, lodges in the bark of a nearby tree, where it begins to grow. The pine I climbed stood alone in the middle of a meadow, a hundred feet from the nearest tree. A bird or squirrel most likely bridged that open space, carrying a sticky seed from another pine on its feathers or fur.

In return, dwarf mistletoe creates new habitat for these unwitting carriers. Blue and sharp-tailed grouse find dense cover in the bushy witch's brooms. Squirrels and raptors nest on their wide, matted platforms, and porcupines eat their tender shoots.

At about forty feet above the ground, my climb ended. Waves of vertigo had been gathering force over the last several feet, and by the time I stopped climbing, they had made putty of my muscles. I wedged myself between two of the main leader trunks and settled back in the safety of the pine's embrace.

Though only a slight breeze stirred the pine's needles, I could hear their whispered roar like a faraway, fast-flowing river. In the soft glow of afternoon light, long needles traced arcs across the sky and glistened as if misted with water. In the days before such romantic descriptions were taboo in biological circles, Donald Culross Peattie wrote:

> When the wind is still and the trees stand motionless in the dry heat, a star of sunlight blazes fixedly in the heart of each strong terminal tuft of needles. Each tree bears a hundred such stars, each clump of Yellow Pines a thousand, and the whole grove blazes like a temple with lighted sconces for some sacred day.

Nestled like a flying squirrel in the lap of the pine, I had the finest seat in that temple, suspended midway between earth and sky on a living column of light.

Just beyond arm's reach, a few cones, open and empty of seeds, still clung to twig tips. Most had fallen, scattered like apples in the sun-softened snow. Whenever I walk among ponderosa pines I invariably pick up their cones. I seek out the hard, mahogany-colored cones to wrap my fingers around as I walk. Each cone is a study in geometric precision, the diamond-shaped scales fitting together in perfect spirals.

Every three to five years, the ponderosa pine produces a dense crop of male and female cones. In springtime, ripe staminate cones swell with pollen grains. Each grain is a small balloon, one-tenth of a millimeter long with two air-filled bladders to send it aloft. When wind sweeps through the trees, pollen grains shake loose from their cones like gold dust and float through the pine forest.

Meanwhile, the female cone develops into a tiny, soft, green version of its mature form. Before pollination, its scales hang open slightly. A tacky fluid in the crevice behind each scale traps drifting pollen grains. The cone then absorbs the fluid, drawing the pollen down to two ovules at the base of each scale. When pollen has fertilized most ovules in the cone, the scales swell closed, sealing in the seeds until they are fully developed a year and a half later.

To protect its precious seeds from predators until they have ripened, each scale is armed with a long, tan-colored prickle. The thin ends of these prickles break off easily, a lesson painfully learned when I tried to pick an immature cone from a low-hanging branch. Each scale in the central portion of the cone shields two small seeds. When the cones are ripe, the scales open outward, lowering their daggers and exposing the winged seeds to the wind.

Ponderosa pines produce cones after as little as sixteen years of growth. I've seen pines no more than nine feet tall and an inch in diameter clutching a single small cone at the tip of a high branch. They continue producing viable seeds for over 350 years, though the seeds from trees between 60 and 160 years old grow best. Each cone bears roughly seventy-five viable seeds, and an average mature pine in a good cone year bears two hundred cones. Yet for all the winged seeds this climbing pine had sown over the years, not a single seedling had sprouted nearby.

Animals likely ate many of the seeds. Ruffed grouse, quail, Clark's nutcrackers, chipmunks, and squirrels rely on the pea-sized seeds for autumn food. On every walk I've taken through pine groves in western Montana, I've found logs and rocks covered with scales and cone cobs where red squirrels have picked seeds from cached ponderosa pine cones.

Many pine seeds remain uneaten, but their chances of sprouting and growing to maturity are slim. Even if they do settle into a sheltered patch of soil and take root, most soon die from lack of water. The seedlings set taproots quickly; after a year, a three-inch seedling tops a two-foot taproot. But two feet means little in sandy soil, and unless seedlings receive adequate water when they take root in autumn, as well as during the following spring and summer, they will die. Because their arid habitat rarely meets these requirements, many years may pass with little regeneration. Around my solitary climbing pine, thick bunchgrass had deterred most seedlings, and lack of shade likely killed the rest.

A seed is in no way assured a long or easy life once it sets its taproot deep in the earth. Usually where one seedling survives, there are dozens of others competing for water, sunlight, and nutrients. Though pines need partial shading for their first several years, they will languish thereafter without sunlight and space. If competition doesn't weaken or kill the young trees, browsing animals might. In the wet snow beneath the pines along Rattle-snake Creek, I found deer tracks leading from seedling to seedling, each cropped of its tender buds.

Among these pines, I searched the fresh-fallen cones for seeds the wind had not yet blown free. Just one-quarter inch long and propelled by an inch-long wing, each seed weighs only one-twentieth of a gram, yet carries the potential to create a tree two hundred feet tall. Gathering a handful of seeds, I tossed them into the air and watched them whirl toward the ground in tight spirals. As they landed on the moist bed of snow and brown needles, I imagined one of them slipping into a sheltered shallow in the soil—surviving squirrels, deer, insects, and fire—and growing as big as the pines I stood beneath, tempting some admirer in a century's time to climb among its sturdy branches.

Robert Petty

3

Moving Across Time

Plants are the youth of the world, vessels of health and vigor, but they grope ever upward toward consciousness; the trees are imperfect men, and seem to bemoan their imprisonment, rooted in the ground.
— Ralph Waldo Emerson

BEHOLD THE YELLOW PINE. In howling gales, it bends and sings. Its leaves glisten like jewels in sun, rain, snow, and ice. Its roots draw nutrients and water from parched earth and provide firm anchorage. Its trunk holds needles one hundred feet in the air where they soak up sunlight unimpeded by competition and transform it to sugar, creating all the food the tree needs. The pine can reproduce on its own, isolated on a rocky outcrop, and it can flourish in a forest of tens of thousands, composing life from earth, air, water, and fire. For more than 250 million years, pines and their conifer ancestors have survived and thrived on earth. *Homo sapiens* evolved a brief 300,000 years ago, and we have searched relentlessly ever since for satisfaction of our basic needs: food, shelter, water, community, and an understanding of our place and purpose on earth, what one might simply call rootedness.

"Trees," Emerson wrote, "are imperfect men." Rather, I say, most humans are imperfect trees, restless and unfulfilled and longing for the stability and self-sufficiency that trees embody. I take issue with Emerson, not so much for his assertion that immobility equals imperfection and imprisonment—though that is arguable enough—as for his assumption that trees are immobile. "To have real rather than sentimental roots is to be in motion," John Hay once wrote, and so it is with the ponderosa pine.

It is easy, of course, to be deceived by the tree's wooden stance. Observe a ponderosa pine on a sandy hillside, its branches motionless in midsummer torpor, and you will find it just where it was last week, last year, exactly where it will stand a hundred years from now. But to call that immobility is to misunderstand the pine's way.

The land surrounding my home in the Escalante Canyon is a labyrinth of sandstone knobs, hoodoos, potholes, and pour-offs. Little grows on these undulating rocklands; there is simply too little sand and water for even the most tenacious seed to take hold. Sagebrush, piñon and juniper, blackbrush and yucca, prickly pear and paintbrush grow in isolated clumps where wind-blown sand has gathered. The effect is that of a cultivated rock garden.

I wandered one afternoon across rolling slickrock between Calf and Boulder Creeks, tributaries of the Escalante, searching for a new way down to the river. A shallow notch that hinted of a drainage cut down to the south, and I rounded a wide sandstone hill to drop into the cleft. There below me, ten miles from the nearest pine, was a magnificent, sixty-foot-tall, burnished yellow pine in a brilliant green bowl of manzanita and serviceberry. A pine sapling, barely ten feet tall, grew beneath the old tree. Yellowed cattail stalks rimming a small, sandy trough recalled wetter times in this tiny oasis. Even in these dry years, though, the sheltered basin collects enough water to sustain the twenty-inch-wide tree and its verdant undergrowth.

I have found ponderosa pines in other seemingly untenable outposts in the canyons—pines growing in no more than a four-foot pothole of sand cupped in a wide sweep of red rock. They are as gnarled and twisted as olive trees, some no taller than I am, though thick roots suggest many years of growing. Each is an elegant bonsai, with rock-pruned roots and wind-bent limbs.

From Powell Point to Boulder Mountain, the Aquarius Plateau curves like a shallow bowl around these slickrock canyonlands. On the steep slopes that rise to the plateau's spruce- and fir-covered highlands, ponderosa pines grow tall and plentiful. Every few years in September and October, the pines set loose a deluge of seeds. On a calm day, the winged seeds fall only a few feet from their parent pine. But given a monsoon gale and a burst of rain-fed runoff, these seeds can travel miles.

Most of the seeds that tumble down the pine-filled slopes to the red-rock swells never take root. Cliff chipmunks and rock squirrels gather cheekfuls of loose seeds and stash them in shallow burrows. Bushy-tailed woodrats hoard others in their rock-pile nests. Thousands more blow into barren crevasses and sun-baked sandslides, wash down slot canyons and beach among coyote willow and cottonwood. It was by sheer good fortune and pure chance that a journey-worn seed found its way from the plateau to my slickrock oasis.

In this roiling, haphazard way, the ponderosa pine has become the most widespread conifer in the West. Ponderosa pines grow from the Frasier River valley in central British Columbia to the Sierra Madres in Durango, Mexico, from Garfield County, Nebraska, to the Pacific coast of Oregon and California. The pine's easternmost limits roughly follow the 100th meridian, the geographic line west of which precipitation drops below twenty inches annually, an aridity that persists until one reaches the lush Pacific Coast. The ponderosa pine has found its niche in these arid lands, occupying the transition zone between piñon-juniper lowlands and spruce-fir mountain forests. Waxy leaves, deep roots, and thick, waterproof bark allow it to thrive in places receiving twelve to twenty inches of rain each year. If the pine takes root in soil overlying shallow bedrock that holds moisture nearer the surface, it can survive in climates with even less rain-

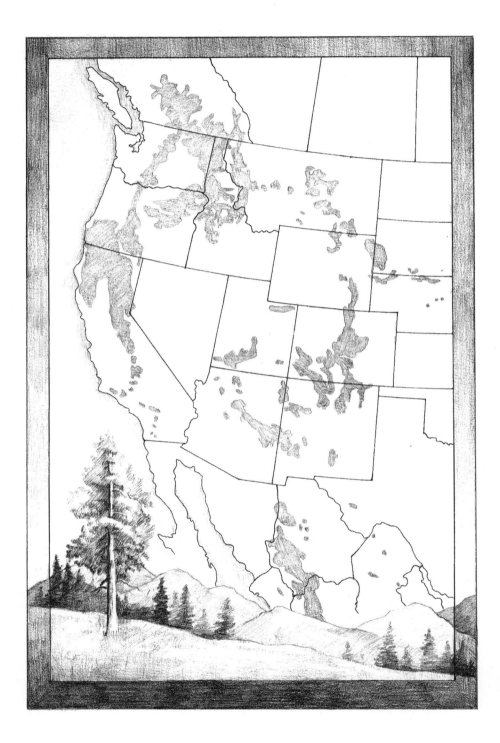

fall. In casting out billions of seeds each year, the pine continually probes the boundaries of its range, settling new ground whenever conditions allow.

But the map of ponderosa pine distribution reveals huge gaps between established stands. In western Texas, one hundred miles of sand-bitten sagebrush lowlands separate the Davis Mountain ponderosa pines from the nearest pines in the Guadalupe and Chisos Mountains. Ponderosa pines cover the slopes of southern Utah's Henry Mountains, yet the closest pine forests are on Boulder Mountain, separated by thirty miles of tortuous, red-rock canyons. Across much of its range, the pine occupies such isolated islands, surrounded by vast oceans of uninhabitable terrain. A million years of wind and water couldn't have carried viable seeds to the sites of these castaway populations.

Their distribution cannot be explained in terms of familiar benchmarks of weeks, years, and decades of growth and change. Understanding ponderosa pine movement demands casting off this frame of reference and thinking like the round earth itself, rolling through the black vault of space for over four billion years. This is no easy transition—centuries are abstractions to us, millennia nearly unthinkable. But ponderosa pines move to the rhythms of glaciers, to the sway of continents that slide and spin across the earth's molten mantle.

Fossils point to Eurasia as the origin of the genus *Pinus*. Ponderosa pine ancestors most likely spread from Eurasia to North America while the two land masses were joined during the Mesozoic Era, 200 million years ago, in the supercontinent Laurasia. During that era, the continents moved apart like scattering billiard balls. North America, at that time located near the equator, drifted northwest at the rate of one-half inch each year, its climate cooling as it went. Its movements forced the Appalachian Mountains from the eastern lowlands as tectonic plates collided. These peaks were weathered remnants of their former selves by the time the Rocky Mountains uplifted 150 million years later. Inland seas spread and receded and spread again. Mammals, birds, flowering plants, and grasses burst from the evolutionary cornucopia, and thousands of species thrived and vanished. Two million years ago, mountains of ice three thousand feet thick advanced from the Arctic southward across North America. Since then four distinct glaciations have occurred, the last just eighteen thousand years ago, with long warming periods in between.

During these millennia of geological transformation, vegetation mirrored climatic changes like a practiced dance partner. As land uplifted, its climate grew colder and its vegetation, through scattered seeds, migrated to lower altitudes. As the earth cooled and glaciers advanced southward, so did plants. Eighteen thousand years ago, conifer forests now found only in Canada grew as far south as Virginia and Tennessee. As the glaciers receded to the north during warming periods, the vegetation followed, gradually reinhabiting the barren rocklands left in the glaciers' wake.

Paleontologists discovered the earliest known record of ponderosa pine in west-central Nevada, in fossils six hundred thousand years old. Since then, pines have crossed and recrossed the West, migrating as temperature and precipitation varied. During cooler periods, ponderosa pines grew at far lower altitudes than they do now. Sediments in Yellowstone National Park hold ponderosa pine fossils more than one hundred thousand years old. The pines no longer grow anywhere within Yellowstone Park; the closest are thirty miles away, in the eastern foothills of Custer National Forest. Recently, researchers found twelve-thousand-year-old ponderosa pine needles in Kings Canyon, California, at a site fifteen hundred feet lower than the pine's present altitude. In the San Andres Mountains of New Mexico, ponderosa pine needles fifteen thousand years old have been discovered in habitat that is now desert grassland.

The islands of ponderosa pine habitat that seem so unlikely and inexplicable result from thousands of years of ebb and flow between climate and vegetation. Mountain populations have become isolated like tidal pools left far from the ocean as it retreats in low tide. But their locations now are by no means static. Today's pine forests are like dancers suspended in mid-leap. Though I am too short-lived to witness more than this seemingly frozen step, the dance continues as steadily as ever. Each generation of seeds expresses anew the inevitability of movement and change. And every seed that pioneers new ground choreographs a new step in the ponderosa pine's journey across the western landscape.

4

Witness Trees: Three Stories

My words are tied in one
With the great mountains,
With the great rocks,
With the great trees,
In one with my body
And my heart.
　　　　　—Tewa Pueblo prayer

I.

IN THE COLD, THIN LIGHT OF EARLY NOVEMBER, I stand on a mesa at the edge of Chaco Canyon in northeast New Mexico. Pale pink and yellow wash the bellies of wind-stretched clouds. Even in the benevolent, gilded glow of early evening, the land beneath looks stark and unyielding, a rough table on which the feast of sky is spread. The canyon is wide and shallow, its cliffs low and unremarkable. Its beauty is muted, held in the textures and hues of dormant vegetation—in the mounded mist of rice grass and rabbitbrush, the angular silhouettes of ephedra, saltbush, and cliffrose, the still-green rosettes of globe mallow clutching stiff, flowerless stalks. It is a land of brown and gray tinged with burgundy, pale green, and yellow.

Chaco Wash cuts the flat canyon floor in a dark, ragged gash. It runs only fitfully, carrying clay-choked runoff in spring and late summer. An average of eight inches of rain falls in this basin annually. No springs trickle from its red-rock walls. A few cottonwoods line the wash; otherwise, the canyon and its surrounding mesas are treeless, offering little fuel for cooking or warmth or shelter.

On the thirty-mile dirt road that leads to the canyon, I pass only a handful of low houses scattered on the land like weathered bones. Last night the temperature dropped to eleven degrees Fahrenheit, and today it is little warmer. I hunch deeper into my coat and turn away from the rasping wind, certain that this is no place for people. Yet, four hundred feet below me, its curved back pressed close to the canyon's north wall, stands the remains of Pueblo Bonito, the largest of a dozen great houses in Chaco Canyon built by the Anasazi Indians nearly a thousand years ago. At its peak, Chaco Canyon was home to an estimated six thousand Anasazi and hub of a cultural network that spanned forty thousand square miles.

Pueblo Bonito, Chetro Ketl, Pueblo Arroyo, and the other great houses of Chaco Canyon are justifiably famous for many things — masterful architectural planning, skillful and beautiful masonry, exquisite turquoise jewelry and carvings, coiled pottery painted with intricate black and white designs, tightly woven yucca and willow baskets. The buildings' size and architectural complexity surpass anything of their kind in North America. Pueblo Bonito alone covers three acres of land and once contained 650 rooms and thirty-three kivas within walls four stories high. In the face of these stunning achievements, it is easy to overlook one of the great houses' most remarkable features — the more than two hundred thousand logs, most of them ponderosa pine, used as beams, lintels, sills, and pilasters to hold the massive buildings together.

After nine hundred years of wind, rain, sun, and ice, the great houses have largely crumbled to rubble. But in the southwest corner of Pueblo Bonito, I find a small, dimly lit room still virtually intact. Several wrist-thick pine logs laid side by side form a lintel over the low doorway to the room. White plaster on the walls has fallen away in places, exposing meticulously laid sandstone masonry. Overhead, two ponderosa pine logs, each a foot thick, span the room's ten-foot width. They are cool and smooth as river stones, resting on three-foot-deep sandstone walls. Laid perpendicular over them are slender pine poles that run the slightly greater length of the room. Hidden above these intermural beams is a layer of juniper shakes topped with shredded bark and, finally, five or six inches of dirt that creates the floor of the room above.

Each of the 650 rooms in Pueblo Bonito had this kind of ceiling, as did all the rooms in the other great houses. Hundreds of circular, ceremonial kivas within the great houses used thousands more pine logs. Their roofs, like those of traditional Navajo hogans, were cribbed. Though most of these roofs have disintegrated, their foundations remain. Walking across a wide courtyard in Pueblo Bonito, I come upon the remains of a subterranean kiva thirty feet wide and ten feet deep. Built into a low stone bench that runs the inner perimeter of the circular room are eight, evenly spaced wood-and-masonry supports called pilasters. The Anasazi laid logs from pilaster to pilaster, forming an octagon. These logs then supported another octagon of slightly smaller logs, offset so that the butt-ends of these logs rested on the midsections of the logs beneath them, and so on until only a small opening for an entrance ladder and smoke hole remained.

The log roof was then covered with enough dirt to bring it to the same level as the rest of the courtyard, so that, from the outside, all that remained visible of the kiva was its ladder protruding from the entrance hole. Inside, the overlaying of three or four hundred pine logs created a ceiling domed like the sky itself, resting on walls circular like the earth's horizon. Within this dark, womblike microcosm, the Anasazi performed rituals, shared stories, and celebrated the earth's abundance and beauty.

In the great kiva of Chetro Ketl, sixty-two feet in diameter, Anasazi builders used four massive ponderosa pine logs standing erect in stone-lined pits as roof supports, allowing a higher, flatter ceiling. Part of one of these supports remained when archeologists excavated the kiva in 1927; the log was nearly twenty-seven inches in diameter.

A fresh-cut pine log twenty-seven inches thick and fourteen feet long weighs more than a ton. The Anasazi had neither pack animals nor the wheel to make transportation easier, so carrying such a log even a short distance would have been a Herculean task. But ponderosa pine stands are far more than a short distance from Chaco Canyon—the closest are fifty miles away, in the Chuska Mountains to the west and on Mount Taylor to the southeast. Fifty miles, that is, as the raven flies. Traveled on foot, the distance is even greater, since the terrain undulates over sheer escarpments, steep arroyos, and rocky ridgetops.

Because it seemed so unlikely that the Anasazi carried the huge pine beams that far, archeologists assumed until recently that the climate in Chaco Canyon had been cooler and wetter when the Anasazi inhabited it, that pines had once grown much nearer, perhaps even within, the canyon. An unlikely source proved this theory wrong. Scattered throughout the rocky slopes of Chaco Canyon and its side canyons and mesas are the bulky nests of woodrats, more commonly known as packrats. The nickname comes from the packrat's habit of gathering twigs, nuts, fruits, seeds, and berries and stashing them at its nest, usually tucked in a rock crevice. Since they also tend to urinate and defecate at these nest sites, and since packrats often occupy the same nest over thousands of generations, an enormous, sticky concretion eventually accumulates that holds a precise record of the plant life surrounding the nest site. Some packrat middens, as biologists call these piles, date back forty thousand years. The middens in Chaco Canyon reveal that the canyon has been a shrub grassland for the past 10,600 years, treeless except for a small number of junipers that the Anasazi likely used up early on.

With the climatic change theory shaken,[1] the inconceivable became plausible—that the Anasazi cut the pines with stone axes in mountains fifty miles away, then hauled them by hand over rocky escarpments and deep arroyos to the building sites. None of the logs studied in Chaco Canyon bear longitudinal scars from being dragged overland, nor compression bruises from rolling or floating in rocky runoff streams, so the Anasazi likely carried them the entire way. Perhaps they peeled the pine logs and left them to dry for a season or two to lighten their load. Perhaps several pairs of men spaced along the length of the log used hide straps to transport the logs, or maybe they simply carried the logs on their shoulders. The details of their efforts are lost — archeologists can only fill in the gaps with best guesses. I gladly return to the comfort of my car after just four miles of walking, burdenless, in the cold winds that shear these open mesas, knowing that none of these rational explanations lessens the enormity of the feat.

What did make their task easier was the network of over four hundred miles of roads radiating from Chaco Canyon to outlying Anasazi communities. These roadways were no crude, meandering trails — they averaged thirty feet wide, laid out arrow-straight on the landscape regardless of terrain. When a road traversed an escarpment, the Chacoans made rock-pile ramps or carved wide staircases into the cliffs. Most of the roadways are now invisible to the untrained eye, obscured by vegetation and windblown sand. But on the mesa above Pueblo Bonito and Chetro Ketl, the grand Jackson Stairway shows clearly in the low light of evening, its edges worn smooth by centuries of runoff.

Though the roads' straight lines seem sometimes to take the path of greatest resistance instead of following the landscape's easier contours, they significantly ease the difficulty of walking. One researcher found that walking on the ancient roads — even as

---

[1]   I hesitate to say "disproven" since archeological theories continually evolve. A group of archeologists is now exploring the possibility that Chacoans actually grew ponderosa pines as a crop in moist depressions in the canyon. These depressions are beyond the two-hundred-foot home range of the cliff-dwelling packrats, which might explain the absence of pine pollen in midden records.

overgrown as they now are — requires thirty-eight percent less energy than walking off the road. During the height of Chacoan culture, when the roads were clear and smooth, the energy savings would have been even greater.

Two of the eight known roadway systems extend to the remains of outlying villages near the ponderosa pine forests of the Chuska Mountains and Mount Taylor. Since discovering these roadways and outliers in the 1970s, archeologists have entertained another theory — that perhaps instead of walking all the way from Chaco Canyon to the pine forests, cutting the trees and hauling them back, Chacoans actually ordered specific widths and lengths of pine wood from woodcutters in these outlying villages, who then delivered it to Chaco Canyon.

The great houses' pine beams support the idea of carefully, rather than randomly, chosen logs. The primary beams are mostly between ten and fourteen inches in diameter, the secondary beams between three and four inches. None of the beams bear natural fire scars — the builders may have cut away scarred sections or the loggers might simply have avoided felling scarred trees.

Like many of the theories concerning daily Chacoan life, theories about the origin and transport of Chaco Canyon's pine logs are largely well-considered, imaginative conjecture. Most will never be firmly proven or disproven. Others will crumble or solidify with new discoveries or new interpretations of old evidence. In examining the ruins, archeologists must assume that every chard, every rock, every feature in the landscape is or may someday be significant to understanding the Chacoan culture.

Early archeologists, surrounded with the dazzling discoveries of pottery, baskets, jewelry, and burial sites, saw little value in the great houses' plentiful, weathered-pine logs. Between 1896 and 1899, members of the Hyde Exploring Expedition, led by Richard Wetherill, made the first archeological exploration of Pueblo Bonito, excavating 190 of its rooms. During that time, they cut up and burned hundreds of pine beams for cooking and warmth. Wetherill and his wife, Marietta, removed others to construct a home beside the ruin.

Then, in 1922, while researching the effects of sunspot activity on the earth's weather, astronomer Andrew Ellicott Douglas inadvertently discovered that the old beams held the key to one of Chaco Canyon's long-standing and much-debated mysteries. Since sunspots occur on roughly an eleven-year cycle, Douglas examined tree rings to see if annual growth fluctuated in response to these cycles. He began with a tree whose age and date of cutting he knew and overlapped its growth ring pattern with the core of an older tree of unknown sprouting and cutting dates. Repeating this procedure with progressively older pieces of wood, he was able to painstakingly create a tree ring chronology that dated back to the sixth century A.D. Until his discovery, archeologists could only dream of knowing the exact age or construction chronology of the ruins. On the day he bridged the final gap in his time line, Douglas knew with certainty that Chacoans cut Pueblo Bonito's first beam in A.D. 919 from a tree 219 years old when cut, and that Pueblo Bonito reached its pinnacle in 1067 and was still occupied in 1127.

In Pueblo Bonito, some of the pine beams' ends are so smooth and straight-edged that their cuts are difficult to distinguish from more modern, metal-sawn cuts. Before raising a beam into place on a wall, builders carefully dressed the log, smoothing ax marks by rubbing the butt ends flat with a piece of sandstone. In many of the masonry-surrounded logs that formed kiva pilasters, builders carved fist-sized cups in which they placed turquoise beads, pendants, and shells before laying the first roof beams. Such details reflect a respect for both the wood and the structure being created—details rendered, not for utility, but for the sake of beauty.

Structurally, archeologists say, Chacoan builders used far more wood than necessary. Since stone was readily obtainable from rocky ledges within the canyon, Chacoans could easily have saved much time and effort by substituting stone slabs for the thousands of wood lintels, sills, and pilasters in the great houses. Why, then, such excesses? Running my fingers over the glossy surface of a sheltered lintel post, I sense that the builders recognized the necessary beauty in the contrast of rough, angular stones against the silken curve of pine logs and knew that their lives would be richer for including this hard-won prize of the mountains.

The logs' growth rings show that a drought began in the San Juan basin in A.D. 1130 and lasted fifty years. Normally scant rains became even more so. Though the Chacoans were remarkably skilled irrigators and farmers, and had created a complex system of canals and floodgates in the canyon to grow corn, beans, and squash, they reached the limits of their ability to manipulate the environment in this new, dry period. Crops failed or yielded little, and Chacoans likely exhausted the basin's drought-reduced supply of wild fruits, nuts, and game. In 1132, axmen felled the last pines for the Chaco Canyon great houses. A few years later, Chacoans began to leave the canyon, dispersing in small groups to find more promising land. By 1150, the great houses were empty.

That the brilliant Chacoan culture dissolved a scant two centuries after it began surprises me far less than that it flourished here at all. What ancient visionaries wandered these withered mesas, stopped at the rim of Chaco Canyon, and decreed, like Brigham Young gazing upon the desolate Salt Lake valley, that this was the place? Surely they comprehended the folly of their efforts, the inevitability of their demise in this barren land.

But these are assumptions of hindsight. The scale of their great houses suggests firm confidence in their ability to wring abundance from the soil. The pine beams alone, strung now like naked ribs between roofless walls, embody the optimism and boundless energy of a culture sure of its permanence. The Chacoan people were, in this way, no different from any other.

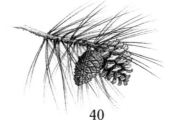

II.

Hanging in the main foyer of the county court house in Missoula, Montana, are eight murals depicting various events in Montana history, painted by Edgar S. Paxson in 1912. In the seventh painting, Governor Isaac Stevens stands by a table in a pine grove with a group of men that includes Chief Victor of the Salish tribe, Chief Michel of the Kootenai, and Chief Alexander of the Pend d'Oreille. Behind them, against a backdrop of tall ponderosa pines and white tents, sit somber tribal members. The scene took place on July 16, 1855, in what is now called Council Grove, and the tribes had gathered to sign the Hellgate Treaty with the United States government.

On that midsummer day in 1855, these chiefs signed away 23,000 square miles of ancestral lands, including all the land between the Continental Divide and the Montana-Idaho border and between the United States-Canada boundary and Lost Trail Pass at the southern end of the Bitterroot Valley. In exchange the tribes received the Flathead Reservation — 2,000 square miles in the Jocko and Mission Valleys — and $120,000 paid over a twenty-year period. One hundred forty years ago, hundreds of people gathered in Council Grove and witnessed the official end of a traditional way of life for Native Americans of western Montana. Now only the pines remain.

Other Montana ponderosa pines offer more visible connections to the old ways of the Salish and Kootenai. At the southern end of the Bitterroot Valley is a campground called Indian Trees. Dozens of yellowbelly ponderosa pines grow here, many of which have four- and five-foot elliptical scars on one side. At first glance, they look like fire scars, but they are not blackened and rarely extend all the way to the ground.

On September 12, 1805, as the Lewis and Clark expedition paused along Lolo Creek on its journey over the Bitterroot Mountains, William Clark noted, "On this roade and particularly this Creek the Indians have pealed a number of Pine for the under bark

41

which they eate at certain Seasons of the year, I am told in Spring they make use of this bark." Pines in western Montana, from the Bitterroot Mountains to Flathead Lake, bear the scars of this practice, formed by Salish and Kootenai women who peeled ponderosa pine bark to gather the sweet, juicy inner cambium.

Each spring from childhood until her death in 1989, Agnes Vanderburg, a Salish tribal elder, helped peel bark from ponderosa pines and cottonwoods. Agnes lived in Arlee, Montana, on the Flathead Reservation and, with the help of her granddaughter Ruby, taught traditional Salish crafts and skills at her camp in the Jocko Valley from late spring to early fall. When I met with her in her home, Agnes, then eighty-eight years old, described the peeling process.

"They peel only half the tree, you know, so they don't kill the tree." Reaching over to a table beside her she pulled out an unopened envelope and a pen. She turned the envelope over and slowly drew two parallel lines on it about an inch apart. "This is the tree, you know. They cut a piece like this on one side." She sketched a long rectangle on the trunk. "Then they put whatever tool they've got under the bark here and pull the bark right off," she said, pointing to the upper edge of the rectangle.

She looked at me for a moment. Her eyes were framed by brown plastic glasses and gray-white hair drawn in two thin braids down her back. Her face, like knotted wood, creased with lines that stretched and curled when she spoke or smiled.

"When they get the bark off, they scrape it," she continued. Using a paring knife from her side table, she opened the sealed edge of the envelope. "They scrape it like this, you see? It's real juicy and sweet."

Timing of the bark gathering was critical. Like maple sap, pine sap has a limited season during which it flows clear and sweet; when that season passes, the sap becomes bitter and cloudy. In springtime, usually in early May, Salish and Kootenai women held a ceremony to determine whether or not the pines were ready for peeling. One woman dug up the root of a bitterroot plant to see if it was ripe for harvesting. If it was, the women went ahead and peeled the pines; if not, they waited. To strip the pines before the roots were ready was considered bad luck. Because sugar content in the sap varies from pine to pine, the women tested each pine's sap before peeling it to make sure it was good.

Peeling the bark was traditionally women's work—mainly strong, young women's work, since the three- to four-inch bark was difficult to peel off and a bark slab could weigh well over a hundred pounds. Agnes and Ruby used kitchen knives to scrape the cambium from the outer bark, but women once used scrapers made of bighorn sheep's horn. They softened the horn by boiling, then carved it into thin, sharp-edged wedges that hardened as they cooled. When white settlers came to western Montana in the late 1800s, they brought tinned food with them, and the Salish and Kootenai began making their scrapers of flattened pieces of metal.

After peeling the pine, the women cut the cambium into smaller strips which they rolled into balls and wrapped with green leaves before storing in cedar bark baskets. Agnes stored the inner bark in a glass jar in her refrigerator.

Few tribal members still peel ponderosa pines. Most peeling ended around 1910, when forest officials, with the support of the Indian Council, barred the practice on the theory that the scars it created lowered the trees' timber value. White sugar soon replaced ponderosa pine bark as a source of sweetness.

According to the journals of Lewis and Clark, and later David Douglas, the Salish, Kootenai, and Nez Percé also ate the seeds of the ponderosa pine. While in the Bitterroot Mountains, Lewis wrote:

> Near this camp I observed many pine trees which appear to
> have been cut down . . . which [the Indians] inform us was done
> in order to collect the seed of the long leafed pine which in those
> moments of distress also furnishes the article of food; the seed of
> this species is about the size and much the shape of the large
> sunflower; they are nutricious [sic] and not unpleasant when
> roasted or boiled.

The seeds are, in fact, quite good, like a small version of the piñon pine seed. They are tedious to shell though, and Agnes recalled gathering as a child only the larger seeds of the whitebark pine from the nearby Mission Mountains.

Although tribal members seldom use the pine as a source of food anymore, they still use certain ponderosa pines as sources of healing, both spiritual and physical. One pine honored by the Salish and Kootenai stands within a few feet of U.S. Highway 93 on the east side of the Bitterroot Valley, between the towns of Darby and Sula. This pine, called the Ram's Horn Tree, was described in many early journals, including that of Hudson Bay Company trader Alexander Ross, who wrote this entry on March 11, 1824:

> Out of one of the pines . . . and about five feet from the ground, is growing up with the tree a ram's head, with the horns still attached to it: . . . almost the horn of one of the horns, and more than half of the head is buried in the tree; but most of the other horn, and part of the head protrudes out at least a foot.

According to local accounts, a white settler cut the protruding tip of the ram's horn from the tree during the 1890s. In the century since then, the pine has grown over the embedded horn. Without tangible evidence, skeptics have questioned whether the venerated pine is, in fact, the original medicine tree described in early journals. But samples collected from a scar on the pine's north side attest to the presence of sheep's horn within the tree. For Salish, Nez Percé, and Kootenai tribal members, the pine offers good medicine and good luck to those who earnestly seek it by making the pine meaningful offerings. Twice a year, Agnes traveled with younger members of the Salish tribe to the Ram's Horn Tree. "Once in the spring takes care of us for the summer. Once in the fall takes care of us for the winter," she said.

The pine's power to heal and bring good fortune is intertwined with the story of how it came into being, retold in this version around 1920:

One day while the Coyote was traveling, he accidently stepped on something which cried out painfully, "Oh, you have broken my leg! I was just about warning you of some danger of which you are almost within reach. But as you have injured me, I will not."

As the Coyote looked down, he saw a poor little lark with a broken leg. "I did not mean it," said the Coyote pitifully. "Do not worry, I will heal it for you," so he did so magically.

"Well now, listen," said the lark. "A little ways farther on you will hear someone calling you. It is the Mountain Sheep Buck, who kills everyone who goes by, as he is very quick and powerful, and when you meet him you must be very watchful, for he may kill you."

"Thank you," said the Coyote, "I will see if I don't put an end to that wicked beast." And so Coyote went on and a little ways farther he heard someone calling, "Coyote come this way." He went on until he saw the Mountain Sheep Buck coming down to meet him. They both walked up to each other until they were very close together, then they stood watching each other closely.

The Buck said in a warning voice, "What right have you to tread over my private land without my consent? Whoever does so, it will cost him his life." "Is that so," said the Coyote, "and have you killed many already?" "Certainly," said the Mountain Sheep Buck, "countless numbers of them." "Is that so," said the Coyote, "you must be very powerful." "Certainly I am," said the Mountain Sheep Buck. "Well," said the Coyote, "let me see how powerful you are with those horns. Strike this pine and let me see how deep they will go into it."

During all this time, the Coyote had his eyes pretty close. "All right," said the Mountain Sheep Buck, and suddenly jumped up and struck for it, and struck it way high above the trunk with one of his horns deep into the tree, and before he could get himself off, the Coyote was right there, holding fast to the tree.

The next moment Coyote drew his great flint knife and cut off the head of the Mountain Sheep Buck, and the body dropped to the ground. Then he cut off the head from the horns which

46

were stuck in the tree, then the head dropped to the ground. He took the head and body and threw them up on the hillside. They splashed on the rocks and they only left a print carved on the rocks—a human face, looking towards the horn stuck in the tree. After this was done, the Coyote stood by the tree and said, "In the future generations this tree will be a Medicine Tree to all tribes."

Agnes described how the Salish also used the ponderosa pine for physical medicine. She said, "When a person's feeling not so good, they take a piece of the tree and bring it in the sweathouse. The person that pours the water, they put the piece in the steam. The needles get hot, like wires. The person hits their body like this." She flicked her hand, holding an imaginary spray of needles, over her shoulder and down her arm. "It helps aches. After the sweathouse, they put the piece over the door. The person that poured the water burns the piece later."

In his journal entry on June 5, 1806, Meriwether Lewis described another medicinal use for ponderosa pine: "I applied a plaster of sarve [salve] made of the rozen of the long leafed pine, Beaswax and Bears oil mixed, which has subsided the inflomation entirely."

Anthropologist Harry Holbert Turney-High wrote in 1937 that Flathead women drank ponderosa pine bark extract to induce labor:

> One of the first medicines the midwife administered was the powdered bark of a pine tree which had been loosened from the tree by a lightning bolt. . . . This was given to the patient in the form of a hot tea and its purpose was to hasten the delivery.

Agnes dismissed this account, however. "Oh, well, people—they like to tell stories. I've never heard that."

"One thing though," she said. "My mother, she used to take the new buds off the tree. She peeled them like this"—Agnes motioned with her fingers—"until she got to the green. She'd

47

take a piece of buckskin and put the buds on it and . . ." She twisted her fist as if grinding with a pestle. "Then she'd add beargrease. You'd use Vaseline now," she said with a grin.

"And what did she use it for?"

"For her hair," Agnes said, touching her head with her finger-tips. "For shine."

The following spring Agnes Vanderburg died. Sitting on the sandy bank of the Clark Fork River where it slides past Council Grove, I peel a pine bud the way Agnes described. Beneath sticky brown scales lie the soft, yellow-green beginnings of a new year's needles. Tacky juices ooze from the bud as I roll it between my fingers. Their scent reminds me of wild pears and lingers long after I return to town.

III.

His four-wheel drive van groans as Leroy Jackson eases it over the muddy, cratered logging road that winds near his summer hogan. We lurch to a stop midway up a rocky incline and then climb by foot to the top of a nearby ridge. To the east, sheer, red-rock cliffs rise a thousand feet from their sandy-sloped base, creating the dramatic west flank of the Chuska Mountains in northeast Arizona. A hundred-mile-long forest of ponderosa pines spills down these slopes, surrounds us, and merges with sagebrush lowlands to the west. Soft folds of these rolling hills conceal the sharp cleft of Canyon de Chelly just a few miles away, its upper reaches cloaked in pines. This is, Leroy's wife, Adella, tells me, the most beautiful part of the Navajo Reservation.

Two years ago, this ridge we stand on was part of an ancient ponderosa pine forest, covered with thousands of wide-trunked yellowbellies. Now it is open and stump-covered, the aftermath of a logging operation that removed all but a handful of pines scattered across the hillside. The mature ponderosa pines in this section of the forest are gone.

Since the Navajo Tribal Council established it in 1958, Native Forest Products Industry has been logging the ponderosa pines of these mountains, cutting roughly forty million board feet of old-growth pine each year. In the company's early days, large-diameter pines were abundant, and NFPI loggers could selectively cut the forest, limiting the visual and ecological impact of their work. Now, with the largest pines gone, they must cut more trees from a shrinking forest to reach their quota, leaving wide scars on the landscape.

The timber sale we wander through is just one of dozens covering many thousands of acres in the Chuska Mountains, but it was this cut that made Leroy and Adella take notice of the extent of logging on the reservation. In the spring of 1990, loggers cut most of the ancient pines surrounding their hogan, devastating a once-beautiful sanctuary. The following year, they discovered blue

logging paint on hundreds of the oldest and biggest pines left on the west slope. They learned, too, that many other Navajo, particularly older tribal members, shared their concern for the old pines, and they soon found themselves the unwitting and sometimes reluctant leaders of the first organized opposition to the reservation's logging practices. In 1991, Leroy cofounded Diné (pronounced Dih-NEH) Citizens Against Ruining our Environment, better known by its acronym, DineCARE. Diné is the Navajo term for members of the Navajo nation. Literally translated, it means "the people."

The heated debate that followed has many of the features of any other western resource conflict. They must cut the last big pines, NFPI and the tribal council say, because so many Navajo jobs depend on the timber industry. Unemployment on the reservation hovers around 34 percent, so the three hundred jobs that NFPI provides seem invaluable. Members of DineCARE insist that the forest has other equally important aesthetic and cultural values that logging destroys. As spokesperson for this group, Leroy has drawn the anger of many Navajo tribal members. He has been publicly ridiculed, received death threats, been hung in effigy from Navajo logging trucks.

The controversy may appear to be a classic case of jobs versus trees, of a traditional logging way of life threatened by a modern environmental agenda. But the logging debate on the Navajo reservation makes a powerful twist on this theme. Here, logging is the newcomer that threatens a traditional way of life in these forested mountains. For hundreds of years, Navajo people have lived among these ponderosa pines, celebrated the old trees' sacredness, and sung songs of gratitude for their bounty. Herbalists and medicine people gathered plants and performed traditional ceremonies within the ancient pine stands and passed their knowledge to their descendents by word and example. In the last thirty years, the Navajo timber industry has heavily logged these forests and threatened the intertwined Navajo way of life.

To call the debate an environmental issue is to see only its narrowest aspect. At its heart, it is a cultural issue, a confrontation between old and new, between traditional and progressive tribal members, not only over the appropriate use of the forest, but also over the appropriate way for Navajo people to inhabit the earth.

In May of 1992, five Navajo elders filed an administrative appeal with the United States Interior Board of Indian Appeals, challenging the legality of a timber sale slated for the forest surrounding their homes. Adella's mother was among them. She speaks only the Navajo language and lives in a hogan in the ponderosa pine forest. She gathers plants from the forest to prepare herbal remedies. For her, the ancient trees are spirits—grandfather trees—and are therefore sacred. She is a part of the forest system, Leroy says, like the black bear and the squirrel—as rooted in the land as the pine itself.

She and other traditional Navajo observe a nine-day ceremony each winter, during which certain participants sing, in sequence and from memory, over five hundred songs directed to the mountains and plants and animals. The songs' focus is reciprocity—the belief that when you take from the land, you must make a meaningful offering in return.

That, in Leroy's mind, is the ethic lacking in progressive Navajo people. They take from the land and give nothing in return. Leroy speaks so quietly that I must turn my head to hear him clearly, but his indictment of the modern Navajo is passionate. They would, he says, sell their own people for a little gain. They have traded their hogans for the squat, featureless tract houses erected by the Bureau of Indian Affairs. In these houses, they gain all the conveniences of modern, white society that the hogans lacked—television, refrigeration, electricity, running water, central heating—but sacrifice their connection to the land, becoming as rootless as tumbleweed. They no longer see the sacredness of the other animals and plants that inhabit the land and so are apathetic to their destruction. They have taken the quick and easy paths of peyote and Christianity instead of adhering to Navajo ways. They are, he says, just like white people.

For the most part, the traditional Navajo way of life is a vestige of the past, embodied now in the elders and dying with them. The children of these elders straddle the chasm between old and new ways. Leroy and Adella live during the summer in a remote hogan and during the rest of the year in modern housing. They speak both Navajo and English. Adella practices western medicine as a nursing supervisor for the Indian Health Service; Leroy sells Navajo crafts. They enter the heart of modern bureaucracy—navigating such labyrinthine federal laws as the National Environmental Policy Act and the Endangered Species Act, commenting on environmental impact statements, filing administrative appeals and lawsuits—to defend the integrity of the Navajo landscape and culture.

As we stand among the slash and stumps of the logged hillside, Leroy tells me that, according to traditional Navajo belief, four animals are responsible for sustaining the ponderosa pine forest— turkey, bear, tassel-eared squirrel, and one other. He stops and I wait to hear more of the story, but he says that is all he remembers of it. I turn the fragmented image over in my mind like a precious potsherd, but find nothing to explain it or offer guidance in these wrecked remains of a forest.

Leroy senses the story's value, senses that the future of the forest and the Navajo way of life hinge somehow upon it, but cannot recall the story itself. When Leroy and I return to the Jacksons' home, Adella says that, as far as she knows, red squirrel is the story's fourth animal. From that, I re-create the story—not, perhaps, as the elders told it, but as I have found the forest to be.

Squirrel, turkey, and bear sustain the forest, just as the forest sustains them. Red squirrel and tassel-eared squirrel cache the pine's seeds, retrieving some, forgetting others that sprout in autumn's rain. Turkey and bear paw for insects, nuts, and berries in the needled humus, exposing soil to pine seeds and burying them within it. In return, a fallen pine log protects black bear's den and turkey's low nest and provides haven for ants and beetles and larvae that black bear eats. The ancient pines give nest holes to red squirrel, firm nest branches to tassel-eared squirrel, and seed-filled cones to them both. Within this relationship of reciprocity, the ponderosa pine forest has survived for thousands of years in these mountains. In the fullness of the forest's story rest the seeds of continuity and survival.

On October 9, 1993, Leroy Jackson's body was found wrapped in a blanket in his locked van at an overlook near Tierra Amarilla, New Mexico. Though investigators found blood on the van's interior, as if a struggle had taken place, Leroy bore no obvious signs of injury, and the cause of his death remains uncertain. For family and friends, foul play seems likely, even certain. Only days earlier, Leroy had spoken out at a heated public hearing in Window Rock, Arizona, protesting the BIA's request for an exemption from the Endangered Species Act, which would allow NFPI to log in prime habitat for the threatened Mexican spotted owl. His comments drew threats of violence from loggers and millworkers attending the meeting. At the time of his death, Leroy was scheduled to travel to Washington, D.C., to speak with officials of the Clinton administration about the devastation of the reservation's pine forests.

John Redhouse, a Navajo traditionalist, spoke at Leroy's burial in an ancient pine grove in the Chuska Mountains. "Leroy was no different than the other Diné warriors and patriots who gave their lives. He took a vow to protect the male deity represented by the Chuskas to preserve balance and harmony for the Navajo people. He saw that the Navajo Tribe has not shared this vision, that they have pursued the white man's values. We will continue his struggle. It is a struggle for our destiny and our future."

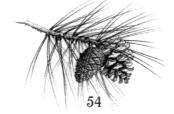

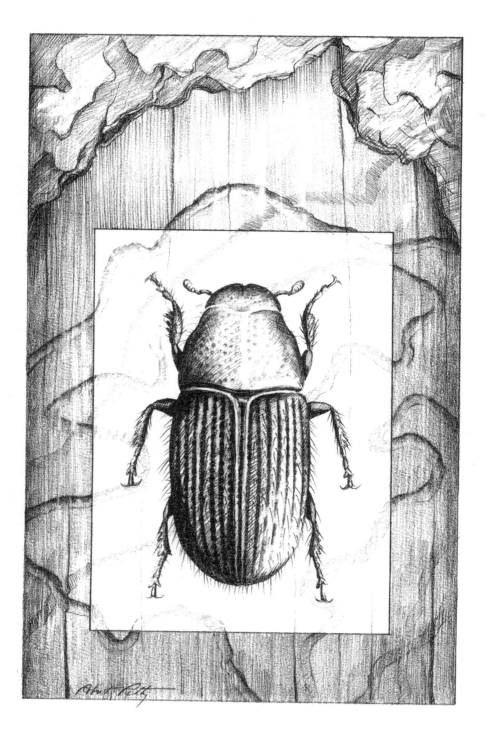

5

Smokey's Legacy

It is the most beautiful region I ever remember to have seen in any part of the world. A vast forest of gigantic pines, intersected frequently with open glades, sprinkled all over with mountains, meadows, and wide savannahs, and covered with the richest grasses, was traversed by our party for many days.
— Lt. Edward Beale, describing northern Arizona in 1857

I DON'T REMEMBER A TIME BEFORE SMOKEY BEAR. Gleaning my earliest memories, I uncover flickers of flame. I hear again the insistent crack and roar of fire as it tears through a cartoon forest on the television screen, snapping at the heels of scrambling fawns and bounding cottontails. A black bear cub shimmies up a seared trunk, separated from its mother, cloaked in smoke and fear, pushed higher and higher by raging flames. Suddenly the fire is over, and somber, unflappable Smokey Bear stands in the forest's smoldering remains. He wears the flat-brimmed ranger hat, work pants, wide belt, and leather boots of the Forest Service and wields a long shovel. His voice is like distant thunder as he intones his mantra, "Remember, only YOU can prevent forest fires." Fires, he says, are bad and unnatural because they destroy the homes, the very lives, of his animal friends. As caring stewards, humans must step in and protect nature against the ravage of flames.

Fire suppression didn't start with Smokey; since its inception in 1905, the Forest Service had been fighting any fires it could and spreading the word that fires were bad. Posters during World War II portrayed forest fires as unequivocally un-American. Slogans like "Careless Matches Aid the Axis" and "Your Match, Their Secret Weapon" underscored pictures of Hirohito and Hitler. But it was Smokey who indoctrinated generations of Americans with the dangers of fire and the need for fire suppression.

Smokey became the symbol of the Forest Service's fire suppression campaign in 1945. His creators had planned to use the less threatening image of a deer as their mascot, but they ran into licensing problems when Disney Productions claimed too great a likeness to Bambi. In 1950, fire fighters discovered an orphaned black bear cub clinging to a charred tree in the aftermath of a fire in New Mexico's Lincoln National Forest. The Forest Service christened the cub Smokey Bear and sent him to the National Zoo as living counterpart to the Smokey legend.

According to a national advertising research report in 1968, Smokey was the best known symbol in America, recognized more often than President Johnson. Today, Smokey's face appears throughout the West on Forest Service land, along with the words "Only YOU" or "Remember." So familiar are we with his slogan that he doesn't need to finish the phrase.

But times and understanding of fire ecology have changed since the Forest Service unveiled the Smokey Bear campaign. Like many scientific and cultural truths, Smokey's view of fire as evil and antithetical to healthy, happy nature is shifting toward a view that better fits our evolving understanding of the natural world. Researchers have discovered that in many ecosystems, including the ponderosa pine forest, fire is a necessary natural process and that a century of fire suppression has done much to harm them.

Most ponderosa pine forests in the West bear the mark of fire suppression. Fire Point, a narrow-necked peninsula on the North Rim of Grand Canyon National Park, is a magnificent exception.

On Fire Point, gnarled piñon pines scribe the canyon's edge, and Gambel oaks grow in scattered clumps in the understory. The rest of the trees, across hundreds of acres, are ponderosa pines. Because Fire Point is so isolated from park facilities, park rangers allow most of its periodic fires to burn. Within this enclave lies a glorious example of a pre-European ponderosa pine ecosystem.

It is not exactly as I expected. Historic photographs and early descriptions of ponderosa pine forests portray endless savannah-like expanses, dotted with widely spaced, massive yellowbellies. Not a seedling or a blackjack pole interrupts the sun-dappled bunchgrass on the forest floor. C. E. Dutton's classic report of 1887, "Physical Geology of the Grand Cañon Region," describes the Kaibab Plateau this way: "The trees are large and noble in aspect and stand widely apart, except in the highest part of the plateau where spruces predominate. Instead of dense thickets where we are shut in by impenetrable foliage, we can look far beyond and see the tree trunks vanishing away like an infinite colonade [*sic*]. The ground is unobstructed and inviting."

This picture is not inaccurate; it is simply narrow. If the old-growth ponderosa pine forest were defined only by old pines, it could not persist. On Fire Point, I find a forest community where snags, fallen logs, seedlings, and blackjack poles punctuate stands of immense yellowbellies, arranged and sculpted by periodic fire.

Thick thunderheads gather along the western horizon. They rise, spread, boil, and roll back upon themselves, darkening like a bruise as they move over the deep canyons, extinguishing light over Kanab Creek, Great Thumb Mesa, Powell Plateau. Ragged forks of lightning connect land and sky in soundless brilliance, shattered by tidal waves of thunder. Wind sings, then screams, up steep escarpments, through thrashing limbs and needles. Another dazzling burst of light, and an old ponderosa pine on Fire Point explodes, hurling stripped bark, limbs, and long flames into the charged air.

In minutes, flames from the blazing pine ignite a dense cluster of spindly poles nearby. Fire rages through the young trees, passing from crown to crown, ripping through their corky bark. Pushed on by hot winds, flames lunge into a stand of mature ponderosa pines, and the fire transforms.

The old pines' shade-pruned trunks are branchless for fifty feet, so the flames cannot reach their vulnerable foliage. Though smoke and heat blacken the lowest needles, their crowns stand clear of damage. Fire sears their bark, but does not penetrate to vulnerable cambium. Flames drop to the forest floor and feed on the dry tinder of fallen needles, cones, and branches. Some trees bear scars from past fires at their bases, and flames lick deep into these. One old pine with a cavernous fire scar cracks in a gust of wind and slams to the earth.

A tongue of flames probes an opening blanketed with waist-high pines. Having lost its momentum and intensity among the big trees, the fire snakes slowly through the saplings, engulfing some, missing others entirely. It meanders on into another stand of mature pines, while the first raindrops hiss on glowing embers.

Wandering among the pines at Fire Point, I find signs of fire everywhere. Every mature tree is singed, the scales of bark around its base outlined in black. When I circle the trees, I find on nearly every trunk a deep, black fire scar. These scars, nick-named "catfaces" for their triangular shape, form when the pine is young and vulnerable. Fire burns hot enough to penetrate the pine's outer bark, usually on the leeward side of the tree where the fire eddies and concentrates its heat. It burns through the tree's cambium and into its heartwood. As long as the wound does not girdle the tree or weaken it so much that it snaps in a storm, the pine will survive.

The fire scar of one old pine tapers from a deep cleft at the tree's base to a point fifteen feet up the trunk. Hardened drops of resin cling to the charred wood, sealing out insects. Another pine bears a neatly domed, foot-high hollow at its base. Once formed, these scars are the old trees' Achilles' heel, the only part of their trunks vulnerable to fire. Every fire that sweeps past a scarred pine will burn its mark into that year's growth ring. A cross-section of these blackened growth rings tells the forest's fire history. The rings reveal that until the 1890s ponderosa pine stands across the West burned every three to fifteen years, with sections burning every year. Lightning started most fires, but local tribes lit many others. In the early 1900s, settlers in Kanab, Utah, reported continual plumes of smoke over the Kaibab Plateau from spring to early fall. Members of the Apache tribe set these fires, both to flush game and to bring rain. These burns also encouraged medicinal and edible plants, like huckleberries, serviceberries, kinnikinnick, camas, and lovage. Bunchgrasses also sprouted profusely after a fire, making good forage for such game as rabbits and elk.

In such frequent fires, no conifer fares so well as the ponderosa pine. Fire strips away the forest floor's thick mat of needles, cones, and twigs and exposes the bare mineral soil in which pine seeds germinate best. Once sprouted, the wispy, seemingly fragile seedlings withstand ground fires better than do the Douglas-firs, white firs, and spruces that compete with them on the plateau. Early on, pine seedlings develop a corky outer bark that protects their cambium and layers of scales that shield moist buds. Since the seedlings drop few needles and produce no cones, the ground beneath them builds up little fuel, and the area is not likely to burn again for at least ten years.

Though I come upon sporadic clusters of seedlings and blackjack poles as I walk among the Fire Point pines, most of the understory is spacious and open, inviting meandering. Donald Culross Peattie wrote of northern Arizona's ponderosa pines, "No conifers are finer than these for a walk beneath their boughs—so ample and wide are their groves, so clean the forest floor of all save needles and grass and pungent sagebrush." Fire created the setting for Peattie's effortless wanderings. Without it, the understory here would quickly fill with competing shrubs and trees.

Having evolved to accommodate and tolerate fire, the ponderosa pine has developed a powerful ally. Fire compensates for many of the pine's potential disadvantages. Unlike most firs and spruces, ponderosa pines are intolerant of shade—young pines will rarely sprout and grow in the full shadow of other trees. Nor are they fully sun tolerant. A seedling must spend roughly half of each day in the shade or its roots will dry out. The small openings that fire creates when it kills a pine here and there in the forest are ideal for ponderosa seedlings. The opening provides the necessary swath of direct sunlight, and the surrounding mature pines give shade early and late in the day.

In one twenty-foot-wide opening, I find more than a hundred knee-high seedlings crowded together. The next fire that sweeps through will kill many of them. But a few may survive, and they will flourish without competition. If all are killed, the cycle will start again with new seedlings until a few manage to survive.

The changes that fire brings to the pine stand on Fire Point are not dramatic. A few scattered old pines die, adding snags and fallen logs to the forest and making room for new pines. Most of the mature trees survive unharmed. The animals living within the forest benefit from these incremental changes. In the hazy light of morning, I spot the white flash of a Kaibab squirrel moving silently through the pine tops. Fungi proliferate beneath fire-thinned blackjack pines, and the Kaibab squirrel thrives on these. A northern flicker drums on a pockmarked snag. Pygmy nuthatches and mountain chickadees flit among blackjack branches, picking insects from bark and needles. Oval droppings and heart-shaped hoofprints betray the passing of mule deer; the twig ends of many seedlings are ragged from their browsing. As I pause in veiled sunlight beneath a yellowbelly, a least chipmunk streaks down a half-fallen log and disappears beneath it. I catch glimpses of these movements as I wander among the pines, my

feet crunching over the thick layer of cones and needles that will
fuel the next fire.

But natural fires no longer burn in most ponderosa pine forests,
as is abundantly clear in lands adjacent to Fire Point. Though these
pine forests are contiguous with those of Fire Point, all part of the
vast Kaibab Plateau, a political boundary separates them. Fire
Point is part of a narrow strip of the plateau along the Grand
Canyon's North Rim that is administered by the Park Service. The
rest of the plateau to the north falls under Forest Service jurisdic-
tion, and it is the policy of Kaibab National Forest managers to
suppress all forest fires. As I step across the cattle guard that
separates Fire Point from Kaibab National Forest, I immediately
see and feel the effects of nearly a century of fire suppression.
What was once a pure pine stand is now a nearly impenetrable

tangle of quaking aspens, New Mexico locusts, buckbrush, white firs, and Douglas-firs beneath mature ponderosa pines. When these yellowbellies die, white firs and Douglas-firs will replace them, since pine seedlings seldom thrive in such dense undergrowth.

Even pine forests with fewer competing species transform in the absence of fire. In Montana's Pattee Canyon, Douglas-firs offer the only significant competition to the pines. Though countless Douglas-fir seedlings and poles crowd parts of the understory, I also find hundreds of ponderosa pine seedlings and saplings in sunny openings. But without fire to thin them, these young trees continue to crowd one another as they grow, forming dense, doghair stands.

The result is predictable. Crowding weakens the pines, inviting infection and disease. More than two hundred species of insects prey on ponderosa pines. Of these, members of the genus *Dendroctonus*, the western bark beetle, kill more pines than do all other insects and diseases combined. Female bark beetles burrow through the corky outer bark to reach the succulent, sugar-laden inner bark, showing strong preference for large-diameter trees whose inner bark is thickest. They then chew a small channel through this layer and lay their eggs along the way. When the eggs hatch, developing larvae eat the inner bark, chewing tunnels that radiate out from the original channel in meandering paths. These channels, though deadly, are often enchantingly beautiful, like delicate strands of seaweed.

If the infestation is small and the tree healthy, the ponderosa pine may be able to produce enough resin to flush out the invading beetles. Like blood, resin flows copiously wherever its ducts are perforated. It drowns the invading beetles and seals out others with a scablike plug, a defense known as a pitch-out. Bark beetles counter this defense by attacking ponderosa pines en masse, gathering together via pheromones. If enough beetles attack a pine at once, the tree will be unable to produce sufficient resin to flush them out, and the resulting larvae will likely girdle and kill the tree.

But *Dendroctonus* beetles are not evil enemies of the ponderosa pine forest. They, like dwarf mistletoe, are members of even the healthiest pine ecosystem, creating habitat for many other animals. Barred and flammulated owls, fishers, martens, wolverines, northern flying squirrels, and pileated woodpeckers nest in the hollows of beetle-killed trees. Woodpeckers feed on the beetles' developing larvae. Fallen logs shelter voles, shrews, and chipmunks and feed new pine growth. But in crowded forests, the beetles' numbers explode, creating an epidemic that can kill tens of thousands of trees.

In Pattee Canyon, fallen logs crisscross the forest floor and lean against living trees. Flammable young Douglas-firs and ponderosa pines fill the understory, creating fuel ladders that allow fire to climb to the crowns of even the tallest trees, potentially killing entire stands.

That is what happened on July 16, 1977, when a fire caused by a downed power line and fanned by high winds swept along the canyon's north-facing slope, leveling six homes and killing every tree in almost twelve hundred acres of forest. Without the rain that came a day later, the fire would have burned far more. Fire scar studies, recording periodic fires for the last four hundred years around the burn site, show no evidence of such devastating fires. The 1977 conflagration was likely the first stand-destroying fire in the canyon's history.

Some trees, like the lodgepole pines of Yellowstone National Park, have adapted to such crowning fires. They grow in doghair stands where trees grow so closely that it is sometimes difficult to push between them. The pines' spindly branches bear two types of cones. One releases winged seeds in autumn, the way most other conifers do. The other is closed tight with pitch and remains on the branch for years. These serotinous cones cast out their seeds only when a fire burns hot enough to melt their pitchy seals.

When a fire starts in this forest, it sweeps from crown to crown, killing every tree in its path until rain or terrain slows its progress. The pines' serotinous cones burst open, casting seeds throughout the burned area. The seeds take root in the newly exposed soil, beginning another doghair stand.

Ponderosa pines cannot reseed the vast open spaces created in a stand-destroying fire. Their cones are not serotinous; when a ponderosa pine burns, its seeds burn as well. On the blackened hillside of Pattee Canyon, fire prepared the soil perfectly for germinating ponderosa seeds, but no mature pines remained to sow them. Even if winged seeds did blow into the heart of the burn, most seedlings would perish without shade. Fifteen years after the fire, bunchgrass, currants, and kinnikinnick grow amid black poles, but the burned area remains treeless.

The campaign to protect ponderosa pine forests from fire began with no less a western authority than John Wesley Powell, who stated in 1879, "The protection of the forests of the entire Arid Region of the United States is reduced to one single problem — Can the forests be saved from fire?" Early forestry reports claimed that the open ponderosa pine stands had been "worn down by the attrition of repeated light fires" that weeded out the best trees. Although a few lone voices championed the benefits of fire and warned against fire suppression, a 1910 report from the Department of Agriculture stated that, if allowed to continue, these "enormously destructive" periodic fires would damage the ponderosa pine forests so extensively that "ultimately there would be no timber at all."

Even before the Forest Service began suppressing fires in earnest, fires in ponderosa pine forests throughout the West began declining in frequency as a result of heavy cattle and sheep grazing. Arizona was no exception. Before settlers introduced livestock, Arizona's pine stands supported an abundance of knee-deep native grasses that were ready tinder for any spark. In 1826, James Pattie camped near Gila Hot Springs and wrote, "The first day we were fatigued by the difficulty of getting through the high grass, which covered the heavily timbered bottom." And in 1858 Edward Beale wrote of northern Arizona: "We came to a glorious forest of lofty pines, through which we have traveled ten miles . . . every foot being covered with the finest grass, and beautiful broad grassy vales extending in every direction." By 1900, cattle and sheep had nearly eliminated the flammable tallgrass species from these forests and promoted grazing-resistant, shortgrass species, such as blue grama and squirreltail, keeping even these stubble-short.

Logging also contributed to the pine forests' transformation and demise. In the late 1800s, settlers built sawmills in the heart of the pine stands and cut the largest of the pines. When the Forest Service formed in 1905 and began managing federally owned forests, it continued the practice of cutting the biggest trees. In the 1950s, the agency launched a program of even-aged management, on the theory that a forest of same-aged pines will, like a neatly sown crop of corn, grow more vigorously and efficiently and yield more lumber than will a forest with trees of many ages. Thousands of acres of ponderosa pine forest on the Kaibab Plateau now form a vast checkerboard of clearcuts in various stages of recovery. Though loggers cut and replanted these areas in the mid-1960s, some are still bare of trees. In others, where the topography and microclimate of the land allowed seedlings to survive without the partial shade of mature trees, saplings grow as thick and even as grass, only shoulder-high after thirty years.

In most ponderosa pine forests, the Forest Service now practices selective thinning, a logging strategy that leaves trees of various ages scattered throughout the cutting area. Though a selectively thinned pine stand appears much less disturbed than one that has been clearcut, its new configuration renders it especially vulnerable to stand-replacing fires. At Fire Point, though ponderosa pines of all ages grow in the forest, they do so in same-aged clusters. This segregation is crucial to the pines' ability to withstand fire. After selective logging, any remaining mature pines stand scattered among seedlings, saplings, and poles. If a fire starts in such a stand, it will climb easily among their stair-stepping crowns and kill many mature trees.

One October afternoon, I climbed Baker Butte fire lookout tower, perched on the Mogollon Rim in north-central Arizona. The Rim, a dramatic two-thousand-foot escarpment of basalt, Kaibab limestone, and Coconino sandstone, forms the southern boundary of the Colorado Plateau. It is also the southern edge of the Mogollon Plateau, which supports the largest continuous ponderosa pine forest in the world, stretching from the San Francisco Peaks near Flagstaff, Arizona, to the Mogollon Mountains of southwest New Mexico. This forest, twenty-five to forty miles wide and three hundred miles long, contains over two million acres of ponderosa pines growing in virtually pure stands.

At 8,074 feet, Baker Butte is the highest point on the Rim and affords a spectacular and telling view of the vast ponderosa pine forest. From the lookout, the Mogollon Plateau stretches in a flat table of green to the eastern horizon. This topography made easy the job of cutting the pines. At the turn of the century, railroad lines transected the plateau and hauled away the large-diameter trees. The forest has been intensively cut ever since. Logging roads riddle the plateau like the meandering borings of a bark beetle.

From the Baker Butte lookout, the plateau is magnificent. Uninterrupted expanses of green suggest a vigorous, healthy forest. Nearly uninterrupted, that is. A black blot along the Rim about four miles east of Baker Butte mars this seamless fabric. A friendly volunteer fire lookout said I was seeing the aftermath of the Bray Fire, the most recent fire in this part of the forest. A real tragedy, she said. She suggested I visit the site so I could see how harmful fire can be.

Forest Service Road No. 300 cuts through the heart of the burn. In the midst of charred poles, I find a large interpretive sign that explains the scene. The fire began on June 4, 1990, from the embers of an unattended campfire. It burned 633 acres of ponderosa pines in the Coconino and Tonto National Forests before firefighters from ten ranger districts could contain it. Taxpayers paid $1,500,000 to fight this fire, the sign says, because of a moment's carelessness. A tragedy, it says, echoing the woman in the lookout tower.

As I wander among the dead trees, I cannot find any trees larger than a foot in diameter. Most are between five and ten inches and are spaced just a few feet apart. These spindly young trees, surrounded as they likely were by slash piles and years of accumulated fuels, were explosives waiting for a spark.

This was not the first stand-destroying fire on the Mogollon Plateau; tens of thousands of acres of pines have burned to charred poles in the past fifty years. The Dudley Lake Fire alone, started in 1956 by a spark from a logging operation, burned 21,000 acres of ponderosa pine. The Dude Fire of 1990 burned 28,000 acres. In the years between these fires, hundreds of others have burned, nearly all to some extent stand-destroying.

Recognizing in the 1960s the fire danger in ponderosa pine forests, the Forest Service began implementing experimental "controlled burns," setting fire to small, closely monitored areas to reduce fuel loads. The name soon changed to "prescribed burns," since control often proved impossible. Fire scar studies of the Coconino National Forest show fire cycles of one to three years until the 1900s. The Forest Service acknowledges that it cannot possibly mimic such burn frequencies and keep up with fuel accumulation. Instead, the agency focuses its attention on those stands closest to developed areas, attempting to reduce the threat to human habitation.

The Bray Fire in and of itself is no tragedy. Knee-high bunchgrasses have thrived, providing habitat for mule deer, elk, mice, cottontails, golden-mantled ground squirrels, and Gambel's quail. As I wade through the grass, faded to autumn gold beneath blackened trunks, three hairy woodpeckers batter the dead trees in search of insects. But this clearing and the fire that created it are symptoms of disequilibrium in the West's ponderosa pine forests. In a balanced, healthy pine stand like that at Fire Point, species dependent on the ponderosa pine for food and shelter can quickly reinhabit the forest after a fire because the basic structure is unchanged; the majority of the pines survive. In the Bray Fire area, it will be at least 125 years before mature ponderosa pines are reestablished, if at all. The animal species that inhabited the pine forest there have been permanently displaced.

"I've something to tell you—a *true* story!" begins the Smokey Bear comic book I find in a Forest Service office in Payson, Arizona. The booklet describes Smokey Bear's traumatic brush with death that precipitated his diligent efforts to stamp out forest fires. But if the comic book story can be called true, it is truth of the narrowest and most simplistic kind, grossly misleading when applied indiscriminately across the country's vastly different forest ecosystems. By misrepresenting the role of fire in natural communities, and by encouraging practices that increase the likelihood of devastating fire, the Forest Service and its mascot bear have contributed to the demise of the ponderosa pine forest. This is the true tragedy of the Bray Fire.

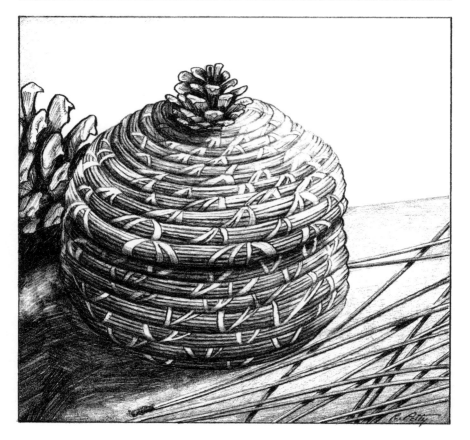

6

Circles of Pine

I too had woven a kind of basket of a delicate texture, but I had not made it worth any one's while to buy them. Yet not the less, in my case, did I think it worth my while to weave them.

—Henry David Thoreau

HEAD BENT OVER MY WORK at the kitchen table, I sit at midnight wrapping the inner coils of a pine needle basket. I hadn't meant to stay up so late, but each new coil lures me on to add another, and each small addition requires careful, patient work. I pause often to admire and smell the cool, spiraling needles.

Across the Clark Fork River from where I sit weaving, the sawmill at White Pine Sash Company, Montana's last millwork plant, is quiet. Until this year, the second-shift millworkers would have just been getting off work, punching their timecards as I clip my last pine needle and store the unfinished basket on the shelf. Now the mill usually runs only a daytime shift, so I am alone in my late-night work with the pine.

Both White Pine Sash and I use the ponderosa pine to craft useful and beautiful things. I make coiled baskets from the pine's needles; the mill makes window sashes from the pine's heartwood. Each process reveals part of the tree's beauty, its curves and straight lines, smooth surfaces and rough.

Pine-needle basketmaking begins in a pine grove in late summer and early fall. There, I gather the fallen, browned needles while they are at their best. After lying under snow all winter, pine needles in spring are often covered with small, black mold spots. By the end of the summer, the pines have dropped a fresh crop of needles, perfect for basketmaking.

I should qualify that, though — not all needles are perfect. In basketmaking, the longer the needles are the better. There's no easy rule for finding long needles. I've seen some immense ponderosas with five-inch needles and others with needles twice as long. Their length seems more dependent on growing conditions than on the age of the tree. Pines in warm, moist, well-drained sites tend to have the longest needles. In Guadalupe Mountains National Park in northwest Texas, I've seen yellowbellies with needles fourteen inches long.

Pines with needles at the shorter end of the scale seem more common, but sometimes in the midst of a short-needled grove, I've found a lone pine surrounded by a bed of long, elegant needles that would bring any pine-needle basketmaker to her knees. To make a grapefruit-sized basket, I gather four or five ounces of needles, a tight bundle about two inches thick.

To find good trees for making sash, the White Pine Sash Company searches out the remaining yellowbelly ponderosa pines of western Montana. Though its name suggests otherwise, the plant mills only ponderosa pine. The original White Pine Sash Company was located in Spokane, Washington, near prime western white pine country. Western white pine yields some of the finest, most easily worked lumber of any western pine and, consequently, was logged heavily in the early part of the century. When White Pine Sash moved its operations to Missoula, where few white pines grow, it kept its name. Top-quality ponderosa pine lumber, which is nearly as light and clear-grained as white pine wood, sometimes goes by the commercial name "ponderosa white pine" or simply "white pine."

Quality, in pine wood, is measured by the number and size of defects—knots, pitch pockets, and rot. The best lumber, "grade B or better," has none of these defects. This wood comes only from the outer layers of a large-diameter pine, usually from the lowest forty to fifty feet of the pine's trunk. Knots form wherever branches stick out from the main trunk, but the pine produces clear-grained wood after the lower branches die and break off.

The wood of young ponderosa pines differs so much in quality from that of slow-growing, mature pines that the timber industry markets it under another name, as if it were from a different species. Fast-growing, young pines, called bull pines, still retain many of their lower branches, so their wood is knotty throughout. After milling, bull pine lumber often twists and warps because the large cells of the juvenile wood are less stable structurally than the more compact cells of mature wood.

I walked through the White Pine Sash mill one afternoon with Duane Duff, the company's vice president of manufacturing. We began in the yard behind the mill where logs between one and four feet in diameter were piled. Pointing over to an open field near the stacked logs, Duane said that in good years those fields were filled with logs for milling. The fields haven't been full in several years; large-diameter ponderosa pines are no longer so easy to come by.

Back in the early 1900s, when three- and four-foot-diameter pines covered the warm, dry slopes of every drainage in the Bitterroot, Mission, and Swan Valleys in western Montana, when ancient trees seemed as common as bunchgrass, settlers logged the big pines with abandon. Many of the trees, with the clear-grained wood for which White Pine Sash searches far and wide, were split for firewood to fuel mills and smelters. The high-quality wood was so plentiful, Duane tells me, that the army used to insist on ammunition boxes made of ponderosa pine wood of grade B or better. Soldiers used the boxes once and then burned them.

In much of western Montana, high-quality pines often require two hundred years to mature. Most clearcutting of mature pines has occurred in the last seventy-five years, so it will be more than a century before new ponderosa pines mature on those lands. But the chances of second-growth trees being left to grow for this long are slim. Logging companies cut their pine stands as soon as they are sellable—in Montana, it takes sixty to a hundred years for a pine to grow to the merchantable diameter of nine inches—so the pines never reach maturity. Though trees are a renewable resource, large-diameter pines, given present logging practices, are not. In spite of the dwindling supply of yellowbellies, the mill still ships out parts for close to a million windows every year, requiring roughly thirty-five hundred truckloads of logs.

As I gather ponderosa pine needles for my baskets, I hold them in bundles with a rubber band around each end to keep them straight. When I am ready to make a basket, I wash the needles in soapy water and then soak a handful in clear water until they are flexible enough to bend without breaking as I wrap the first tight spirals. After several spirals, I can use dry needles without fear of breakage. The needles should not soak too long or they will absorb too much water. When the basket dries, soggy needles shrink and the coils become loose. It is for that reason that I avoid weaving with fresh, green needles. Like a pine grove after a summer rain, the kitchen fills with the sweet scent of resin as the needles soak, a fragrance that lingers for months after the basket is finished and dry.

At White Pine Sash, the pine logs, too, are dropped into water—a large holding pond—before going to the mill. The pond provides an easy, though outdated, way of transporting the logs to the debarking machine, which draws thick-barked trunks from one pond and drops barkless logs into another.

The stripped logs then float to the first mill saw, called the headrig. As we watched the huge saw slice through a three-foot-diameter log, Duane shouted the prices that each cut piece would bring when fully machined. "That's $1,900 per thousand board feet right there," he called out as the screaming headrig sliced off a flawless piece. The air was thick with pine scent. The next piece showed a few lines of pitch where the tree may have been damaged by insects. "Now we're down to $1,500." The center of the log, worth the least, was cut for two-by-fours, to be sold for construction work. Some of the centers of the old pines were dark and rotted; these went to another machine to be ground into sawdust.

Milling works from the outside in; each cut of the saw unveils heartwood closer to the tree's core. It is a process of making curves straight, of making rounded edges angular. To create sashes, the mill reduces the original several-ton log into hundreds of straight, smooth-sided, identically shaped boards. Of all Montana softwoods still abundant enough to log commercially, ponderosa pine yields best to this manipulation, not splintering or cracking the way other woods, like Douglas-fir and western hemlock, often do.

Weaving a coiled basket works from the center of the circle, spiraling outward. I work new needles in gradually, tucking their ends inside the coil, each needle merging with the one before it to form a single, continuous spiral. Hundreds of straight needles form one round basket; the whole is greater than its individual parts. Concentric bands radiate from the center like growth rings in a pine's heartwood. The basket's shape emerges as I make it; the finished piece is always a surprise.

Each creating process involves motions performed over and over in practiced sequence. I thread a soaked piece of raffia, a plant fiber that binds the pine needles in place, on my sewing needle and push it through the coil where I left off, wrapping the raffia around the loose pine needles at the coil's end. Back through the coil beneath and around again, a little farther ahead this time, and so on. My fingers ache from pulling the needle through tight coils, my neck from bending over so intently. I add new needles as the loose end thins; the spiral slowly grows. I look up from my work once, and the clock reads nine o'clock; again a moment later, and it is past eleven.

White Pine Sash, too, runs on repetition of movements. Each person does a single job, some for as many as forty years; movements are steady and mechanical. At one side of a warehouse, workers stand by table saws that they operate by pressing a button with one knee, cutting the knots from long boards and dropping the clear-grained pieces on a conveyor belt that carries them to a revolving circular table. Here, six men and women sort the boards by size, moving quickly, paced by the roll of conveyor belts. Scrap wood glides to the sawdust-making machine; short, clear pieces to the finger-jointing machine. Dollies carry sorted lumber to the final milling rooms from which they emerge as window parts. The entire room rolls in practiced rhythm to the vibrations of droning machinery and whining saws.

I have no illusions that my work fully parallels that of the men and women at White Pine Sash. For me, the repetition is voluntary; I make baskets for the pleasure of making them—the pleasure of gathering the needles on a warm autumn day, of smelling the moist needles in my kitchen sink, of discovering the basket's shape, of creating a beautiful container from a handful of dead needles. Because the baskets take so long to make, I cannot make a living from them. Even done at minimum wage, the baskets would be too expensive for most people, so I give them away as I make them.

White Pine Sash creates products from the ponderosa pine for profit; the workers carry out repetitive motions out of necessity, to earn a living. Though the mill as a whole is involved in the process of transforming a newly cut tree into a nearly finished product (the sashes are sent elsewhere for assembly), each worker participates in only a small fragment of the work and does not see the finished product he or she has helped to create.

As White Pine Sash's supply of logs declines, the milling process becomes even more fragmented. Now that the sawmill runs on only one shift, the mill gets much of its sash lumber precut from other lumber mills, original logs and headrig operators un-

78

known. The assembly-line structure of the mill is undoubtedly more efficient and profitable than if every worker were building sash from raw logs. Yet it sacrifices the sense of fulfillment that comes from beginning and completing a project, a satisfaction that is lost when one performs only one step of the process before passing the work on for others to complete.

Even in my work weaving baskets, I miss out on complete fulfillment in the creating process. In the baskets I have made so far, I have bound the pine needles together with raffia. Not only is the raffia gathered and prepared by someone else, but it also comes, for the most part, from palm trees grown thousands of miles from the nearest ponderosa pine forest. I regret this aspect of my weaving; it diminishes the basket inestimably. I am experimenting with dogbane as weft for my baskets. Also called Indian hemp, dogbane grows in moist places in the West, usually along streams. In winter, after the waist-high stalks have died and cast their seeds for next year's plants, I break them at their bases. Inside a hard outer covering, the stalks are filled with long fibers that, when twisted together, form thread. It is, without question, more work than using raffia, and that is much of its beauty. The pine needle basket woven using Indian hemp will fully reflect the land from which it draws its substance.

Native Americans have woven coiled baskets for at least two thousand years, using such fibers as yucca, willow, sumac, redbud, bullrush, squawgrass, and alder. Coiling with pine needles is a relatively new craft, originating about the time of the Civil War along the southeast coast, habitat of the longleaf pine with its graceful, eighteen-inch needles. It will continue as long as weavers and pines exist, since the craft demands so little of the tree.

Like pine-needle basketry, milling with ponderosa pine is a relatively new craft, practiced only since the mid- to late 1800s. The conveyor belts at Missoula's White Pine Sash have been rolling since 1920. In those days, the heyday of milling in Montana, ponderosa pine was used for making almost anything that required wood—furniture, vehicles, scientific instruments, faucets, saddles, cabinets, and paneling.

Now White Pine Sash is the only one of four original millwork plants left in Montana, the rest out-competed by other building materials and unable to pay competitive labor rates. Milling large-diameter ponderosa pines is a craft that is dying just a century after it began. Big pines are disappearing and, with them, their lengths of clear-grained wood. White Pine Sash recently bought veneering equipment to stretch the amount of flawless sashes they can make from a single big log. These machines can slice off sheets of pine as thin as one-sixteenth of an inch and glue them over knotty or finger-jointed lumber. But the veneer is just that, a thin covering over a deeper problem, and the company foresees switching to other tree species in the future when it can no longer find old ponderosa pines to mill.

In a well-made coil basket, the beginning and end of the coil disappear; the basket spirals outward and back on itself endlessly. The basket mirrors the circular patterns of the tree from which it is made—circles of heartwood, spirals of winged seeds, cycles of growth from seedling to decayed log to new seedlings. As I join the coils of my pine needle basket, I re-create these spiraling patterns and continue the work of centuries of basket weavers who knew and practiced these patterns before me.

7

Gold Creek's Last Stand

"DRIVE SEVEN MILES UP GOLD CREEK ROAD. Just before the bridge over Gold Creek, there's a road to the left. You'll have to park there and ski in. The Primm place is just a mile and a half up that road. You can't miss it," said Chuck Seeley, forester for Champion International.

I drove to Gold Creek one late-March day to find a 160-acre piece of land known as the Primm ranch, where some of the finest old ponderosa pines in western Montana were said to grow. The prospect of finding yellowbelly pines up Gold Creek was intriguing not only because stands of ancient pines are a rarity in Montana, but also because, at the time, most of the Gold Creek drainage was owned by Champion International Corporation, which ran Montana's largest private logging operation. Gold Creek is infamous for its cut-and-run look, with thousands of acres of clearcuts and few seed trees left to promote regeneration.

That timber companies sought out and cut the Gold Creek trees is not surprising. Much of the drainage, up to an altitude of about 4,500 feet, is prime ponderosa pine habitat. Lodgepole pines cover the colder, north-facing slopes, and Douglas-firs and larches grow along the ridgetops and in moist ravines. Until thirty years ago, though, few of the drainage's trees had ever been cut.

In the 1890s, the Big Blackfoot Milling Company began to cut large-diameter ponderosa pines in the lower drainage. These pines grew in mixed stands with Douglas-fir and larch, but loggers cut the pine first because its wood brought the best price of the three. Horse teams then hauled the pine logs down to the Blackfoot River, where they were floated nine miles downstream to the company's mill in Bonner. Because there were no roads up Gold Creek at the time and long-distance hauling of logs overland was difficult, the company's logging operations extended little more than a mile up the drainage.

Anaconda Copper Mining Company bought the Big Blackfoot Milling Company in 1898, including its Gold Creek land holdings. At that time, ponderosa pine wood was in great demand in mining towns, particularly Butte, where the logs fueled copper smelters and formed the lumber for mine timbers, railroad ties, and the many new buildings constructed during the boomtown days. Anaconda Copper used roughly forty million board feet—over eight thousand truckloads—of ponderosa pine timber each year just to maintain the frames in its mine tunnels.

It was at about this time that Frank and Edna Parker homesteaded 160 acres in the upper reaches of the Gold Creek drainage. They built a home there, accessible only by a rough trail nine miles from the Blackfoot River road, sixteen miles from the nearest town of Bonner. They survived by raising potatoes, hay, and beef cattle for market, but found it hard to break even. In 1915, the Parkers mortgaged the ranch for $1,600, and in 1926, they sold the timber rights for all 160 acres to Anaconda Copper. In those years, the trees on their ranch and the thousands of acres of virgin forest surrounding them remained inaccessible to logging crews, walled off by rocky escarpments. Anaconda Copper sporadically considered and abandoned ideas for reaching the trees. At that time, timber companies logged many forests by rail, and Anaconda Copper and other logging companies built thousands of miles of track through Montana's forestlands to retrieve the trees.

The company laid tracks up the first two miles of Gold Creek, but stopped at the foot of impassable cliffs. Several years later, it turned again to Gold Creek, this time with plans to dam the upper drainage and build a flume that would float the logs down to the Blackfoot River. Though the company went as far as drawing up plans for both dam and flume, it eventually scrapped the plan because of its cost and complexity.

In 1938, Frank Parker died, and a Texas couple, Charlie and Mahala Primm, bought the Parker ranch to get away from the dust bowl and settle in the clear-aired northern mountains. Many tales surround the Primms' tumultuous marriage; some say Mahala gave Charlie such a hard time that he hitched a ride to Missoula one day and never returned. However their separation came about, in 1951 Charlie deeded his share of the land to Mahala.

By the late 1950s, Anaconda Copper succeeded in blasting a road up the rocky Gold Creek drainage. Over the next twenty years, the company cut much of the drainage's primeval forests, and in 1972, sold all its timberlands to Champion International, a New York-based corporation. During those years, Mahala lived on the ranch with her only son, Morris, making her living by grazing livestock and harvesting hay in the pine meadow. Morris later moved to Texas, and she continued to live on the ranch alone, without gas, electricity, or running water, snowbound during much of the six-month winter. In the mid-1970s, Mahala became ill, and Morris moved her to a nursing home in Missoula. Though she planned to return to the ranch when she recovered, she died in Missoula in 1977 at age seventy-nine.

Having run into financial problems in the late 1970s, Champion began what it called an "accelerated liquidation program" of its large-diameter trees. In 1978, it boosted its annual Montana cut from 170 million board feet to 240 million board feet. The company continued this accelerated cut until 1986, when it cut—with the exception of the Primm ranch pines—the last of its old-growth trees. Champion was not alone in this decision to cut all remaining ancient trees; most private timber companies—including the state's second largest, Plum Creek—did the same. Together, the two companies own 1.7 million acres of forestlands in western Montana. In 1986 alone, they cut a combined 569 million board feet of timber from these lands. As a result of this program, Champion estimates that less than 1 percent of its 867,000 acres of timberland in Montana are still well stocked with trees greater than nine inches in diameter, the minimum merchantable size.

It was, for those companies, a simple matter of economics. Old trees are a high-risk, low-yield investment. They generally grow more slowly than younger trees and are more vulnerable to diseases and insects. So from a profit perspective, it made sense for the companies to cut the big trees and invest the profits in more lucrative assets.

All along the seven-mile drive up Gold Creek Road I saw signs of the liquidation program. Snow had melted from most of the steep hillsides, exposing vast clearcuts strewn with slash timber and stumps, many three and four feet in diameter. Skid trails and bulldozer bladelines cut wide, parallel grooves down the slopes; runoff erosion etched deep ruts along their paths. Some of the less precipitous logged slopes held scattered seedlings in the broken soil. Most were completely barren, their chances of regeneration dwindling with every soil-washing rainfall.

As Chuck Seeley had promised, I found the closed gate of the logging road to the Primm ranch just before the Gold Creek bridge. I skied slowly up the gentle incline, past thick stands of lodgepole pine, past seedcuts where loggers had left a few pines and Douglas-firs on each acre to sow seeds for regeneration, past wide clearcuts. As I reached and went beyond what seemed at least a mile and a half, I began to think that I had missed a turn somewhere, that one of the intersecting logging roads I had skied past was the road to the Primm ranch.

Then I saw what I could not miss—a stand of tall trees down the hill to my left. From their wide, long-needled crowns, I could see they were ponderosa pines. A path angled down the hill, and I glided slowly into paradise. Reflecting the crisp, early-spring sunlight, roan-colored trunks glowed like embers against the snow. Many of the pines were over four feet in diameter and most stood thirty or more feet apart from one another in the forty-acre meadow. I have heard that the old pine stands were once so spacious that people used to drive their Model Ts through them. At the Primm ranch, such a drive would be effortless.

At least half of the old trees bore deep fire scars on their trunks, carved by centuries of periodic fires. Sun-warmed trunks had melted the snow around them, revealing low-growing kinnikinnick and bunchgrass. Scattered among the old pines were stumps of dead trees that Champion had cut to maintain the stand's manicured, parklike appearance. Though Champion claimed to manage the ranch as a natural scenic area, it was far from natural. There were no snags there, no fallen logs or seedlings. None of the earthy, messy rot and rebirth of an ancient forest. Still, surrounded on all sides by the devastated aftermath of Champion's logging operations, I was amazed that any big pines, dead or alive, remained there at all.

After Mahala died, several groups, particularly The Nature Conservancy and Montana Fish and Game Department (now Montana Fish, Wildlife, and Parks), looked into buying the land and the timber rights to preserve the old trees. A timber cruise performed in the mid-seventies estimated that the forty-acre stand of old pines was worth $225,000 on the stump. Neither the Fish and Game Department nor The Nature Conservancy could afford to buy the land and timber rights, so in 1979 Morris Primm sold the ranch to Champion International.

Had Champion, or earlier, Anaconda Copper, wanted to log the Primm ranch pines, it could have done so at any time after Anaconda bought the timber deed in 1926. When Anaconda Copper built the Gold Creek logging road in 1960, the pines became accessible, and records show that the company planned to harvest them. A 1953 Soil Conservation Service study of the area stated, "The magnificent stand of ponderosa pine on the farm is owned by Anaconda Copper Mining Company which plans to harvest them in the next few years. This will help improve some of the hayland by eliminating pine needles in the hay."[2]

Anaconda Copper may have delayed logging the pines in part because of the abundance of large trees elsewhere. Once Champion cut most of its merchantable timber, the temptation to cut these remaining pines must have been far greater. But Chuck Seeley assured me that Champion remained committed to preserving the area.

Tom Greenwood of Montana Fish, Wildlife, and Parks, who pushed in the late seventies to have the ranch made into a state park, agreed that the pines seemed safe. "They'd be the last trees cut, just before the company closed its doors," he said. In 1993, Champion did close its doors, selling all of its Montana land holdings to Plum Creek Timber Company. As yet, the company has not revealed its plans for the ranch.

At one end of the pine grove I found a scattering of rough-board outbuildings and Mahala Primm's cabin. Rusted wheels, rods, springs, and a chipped enamel tub lay half buried in grass and snow around the sheds. Mounded hay softened the hayloft windowsill of a small, neat barn, incongruous with the ranch's look of long abandonment. The splintered boards on Mahala's porch floor bowed beneath my weight. I pushed on the door and it opened stiffly into a gray-lit, narrow entryway. I entered timidly, half expecting Mahala behind each door, shotgun cocked and aimed. Standing in the doorway of her kitchen, I saw that many had been here before me. Empty cans filled the sink and spilled across the counter; the windows were bullet-riddled. A steep

---

[2] Ponderosa pine needles, if eaten during the last few months of pregnancy, can make cows abort their calves, killing both cow and calf in severe cases.

stairway climbed from one corner of the kitchen to an attic bed-room. Sitting on the top step by a window that overlooked the pine grove, I tried to imagine a life in this lap of beauty and solitude.

On a low hill beyond the house, encircled by a polished metal fence, stood Mahala Primm's gravestone. Though I have never seen a picture of her, I imagine her late in life as pinelike, with deeply furrowed, ruddy skin, and a crown of wispy, wind-tossed hair flashing silver in the sun. Those who met her say she was a strong-willed, outspoken woman who passionately loved this ranch. I like to think that it was, as some people claim, her spirit and devotion to the land that protected the pines and protects them still.

8

Tapestry of
the Ancient Forest

THICK CLOUDS BRUSH THE MOUNTAIN'S WILD HEAD and spill over slate gray escarpments. Big-bellied ponderosa pines wrestle with the wind, their limbs rising and subsiding like ocean waves. Their needles sigh in a whispered roar that is at once unreachably distant and exquisitely intimate. Enveloped in these subtle strains, I walk slowly on a trail in the Santa Catalina Mountains east of Tucson, Arizona, and catch my first glimpse of the most beautiful squirrel on earth.

The suddenness of our meeting startles us both. The squirrel is intent on the ground, digging in the soil, perhaps burying a cache of seeds on this day that smells of winter. He does not see me, nor I him, until we are just a few yards apart. More attentive to the forest than I, he senses me first and leaps to the trunk of a pine with a shrill bark. From a branch twenty feet up, he stops and barks again. A luminous tail—pure white beneath, charcoal gray on top—floats above his body like an apparition, whisking from side to side with each yip. His body mirrors the tail's coloring—white beneath, iron gray tinged with rust on top. He climbs higher, a fluid wave of motion, leaps to a nearby pine, then to another, and dissolves into green.

In his wake, a single, disembodied image remains suspended in my mind like the Cheshire Cat's smile—those magnificent, feathered, two-inch-long ridiculous ears. Adorning his head like great exclamation points, they give him a look of perpetual and comical surprise.

Sciurus aberti, Abert's squirrel, tassel-eared squirrel. No other animal depends so absolutely upon, nor lives on such mutually beneficial terms with, the ponderosa pine. As with any fine, intimate relationship, the one between tassel-eared squirrels and ponderosa pines is complex beyond full comprehension, and from it emanates a wealth of other relationships, like seeds from fertile soil.

Though ponderosa pines grow throughout the West, tassel-eared squirrels inhabit just part of that range—central Colorado, southeastern Utah, Arizona, New Mexico, and central Mexico—limited, it seems, by deep and prolonged snow cover in the north and west. The pine forests in much of this area are isolated islands, surrounded by desert, chaparral, or sagebrush lowlands. The Chuska Mountains, the La Sals, the Abajos, the Santa Catalinas, the San Juans, the Colorado Rockies, the Kaibab Plateau, and the Mogollon Plateau all contain populations of ponderosa pines and tassel-eared squirrels cut off from genetic interchange with other populations for nearly ten thousand years.[3] As the Wisconsin glaciers receded and ponderosa pines retreated to the high mountains and plateaus of the Southwest, the tassel-eared squirrel followed. The result is a classic example of island speciation—the West's own version of Darwin's finches. From the common genetic pool of *Sciurus aberti* came nine distinct subspecies: *Sciurus aberti aberti, S.a. barberi, S.a. durangi, S.a. phaeurus, S.a. chuscensis, S.a. mimus, S.a. ferreus, S.a. navajo,* and *S.a. kaibabensis.* So strikingly different is *S.a. kaibabensis,* the Kaibab squirrel, that it was, until recently, considered a separate species.

The differences among the subspecies are mostly invisible to the casual observer—differences in cranial size, body weight, and

---

[3] Although tassel-eared squirrels thrive in the Santa Catalina and Graham Mountains of Arizona, they were recently introduced, not native, to those areas.

92

the like. But in a few outposts, their variations are beautifully apparent. In the foothills outside Boulder, Colorado, I saw *S. aberti ferreus*, with its ink-black body and snowy, black-topped tail, and on the Grand Canyon's North Rim, the Kaibab squirrel, most exquisite of all. Its thick tail is completely white, brilliant against the forest's earthy tapestry of gold and green.

The differences among the subspecies run deeper than appearances, and correspond with genetic variations among the ponderosa pines. The cambium of each isolated pine population has slightly different terpene composition. Pine cambium is one of the tassel-eared squirrel's primary food sources. Each subspecies of the squirrel has adapted to eating the cambium of its host ponderosa pine population and finds that of other populations unpalatable.

Despite these differences, the subspecies are alike in their dependence on the ponderosa pine. Their entire lives play out beneath the pines' interlocking crowns. From these trees they obtain nearly all their food; among these trees they mate, nest, and die. They know the pines in their home range better than any other creature, each one as familiar as a well-worn path.

In late spring, clusters of stamenate cones on the pines' twig ends swell with pollen. Haggard after a long winter and frenetic mating season, tassel-eared squirrels gorge on the cones, dusting themselves and the forest around them with golden pollen grains. When these wither, the squirrels move on to the sticky, green ovulate cones. From early summer until autumn, tassel-eared squirrels feast on their seeds, a single squirrel working his way through as many as seventy-five cones in one day. In summer they also eat the spongy, yellow shoots of dwarf mistletoe clinging to the pines' branches.

By late July, monsoons arrive in the Southwest. Throughout much of August, blue-sky mornings give way to clouds that build to dark mountains in minutes, shaking tree roots with their thunder, unleashing lightning and wild winds. Some days the clouds yield no more than this stormy show—veils of rain hang loosely from their flanks, evaporating before they reach the ground. Other days, they release a deluge that falls like lead shot. In the redrock canyons, these rains create waterfalls at every pour-off, gather into spectacular and fleeting floods, and vanish downstream. In the ponderosa pine forest, long-needled crowns break the downpour's force, and thick, dry humus drinks deep like a long-dry sponge. After a week of these rains, the forest floor erupts in an explosion of new life, mostly hidden beneath fallen needles.

From a pine thirty feet away appears a splash of white. A tassel-eared squirrel scrambles headfirst down a golden trunk and out onto the forest floor. He stops abruptly—tail poised in a question mark over his back—and digs with his front paws through the humus.

Pushing aside two or three inches of needles, he pulls from the hole what looks, from a distance, like a pale acorn—a creamy white, half-inch, smooth ball, flecked with soil. Hunched on hind legs, he bites into the ball, revealing a chocolate brown interior. Another minute's nibbling and the ball is gone. The squirrel pauses, surveying the forest with quick turns of his head, moves a few feet away, and digs again. Each time he digs, he quickly finds food. His sense of smell is keen, and the food—hypogeous fungi, better known as truffles—deliriously pungent.[4]

I had always thought of truffles as something exotic and rare, borne of moist, deciduous, faraway places, unearthed by immense pigs on rolling French hillsides. Though France boasts the most famous and expensive of truffles, *Tuber melanosporum*, or Perigòrd truffle, hypogeous fungi grow throughout the world. The truffles of the ponderosa pine forest appeal less to the human palate than

---

[4] In more scientifically correct terms, not all hypogeous fungi are considered true truffles, a designation limited to members of the order Tuberales. Other hypogeous fungi are considered false truffles, for various morphological reasons. I will, for simplicity's sake, refer to all as truffles.

does the Perigòrd truffle — at least three species are decidedly poisonous — but they are delectable to the tassel-eared squirrel and essential to the pine.

Like all fungi, truffles lack chlorophyll and so cannot make their own food. Some forest fungi are parasites, feeding on healthy or stressed trees. They create the myriad rots that are bane to foresters, boon to cavity excavators: red heart rot, brown stringy rot, white butt rot, red ring rot, brown cubical pocket rot. Other fungi are saprophytes, feeding only on organic matter already dead. Their names are as striking as their strange and lovely forms — fairy clubs, puff balls, stinkhorns, earth-stars, bird's nest fungi, jelly fungi, toadstools.

Truffles are symbionts; that is, they live in a beneficial, necessary coexistence with their hosts — in this case, the ponderosa pine. The round truffle itself is only part of the fungus, as an apple is only part of the apple tree. White threads trail from a spot on the truffle's underside, like streamers from a balloon, and wrap around the root tips of a nearby pine, forming a dense, enveloping sheath. These threads are collections of hyphae, microscopic rootlike filaments that absorb nutrients and water for the fungus. So completely interwoven do pine root and hyphae become that they are considered a single organ, called *mycorrhiza*, meaning "fungus-root." The hyphae absorb sugar from the pine's roots. The pine's roots absorb water, minerals, growth-regulating B vitamins, and growth stimulants from the hyphae.

This is no small exchange. Hyphae are masters of absorption. Ponderosa pines inhabit arid lands, where the difference between good and superb water-absorbing capabilities can mean the difference between death and life. Without mycorrhizae, ponderosa pines — especially seedlings and saplings, whose roots are shallow and poorly developed — could not survive.

Both ponderosa pines and their symbiotic truffles have evolved to take fullest advantage of monsoon-season moisture. During that time, both truffle spores and pine seeds reach maturity. Soon after

95

they fall to the ground, the pine seeds set hair-thin, fragile roots. The abundant and ubiquitous truffle spores begin forming hyphae around these superficial roots, boosting the seedling's chance of surviving the coming dry seasons.

The truffle itself is an adaptation to arid habitat. Underground, the fruiting body has a better chance of remaining moist long enough to produce mature spores than if it sprouted aboveground. But the buried truffle misses out on a key advantage shared by aboveground fungi—exposure to the wind, which allows easy, efficient spore dispersal.

Enter the tassel-eared squirrel. He can smell the fragrant, moist, mineral-rich truffles through as much as a foot of snow and will gorge on them as long as they last. Fungal spores emerge unharmed from the squirrel's digestive tract, handily embedded in fertilizer. Squirrels defecate on the run, scattering spores through the forest, promoting the survival of both truffle and pine.

While rich autumn foods are abundant, tassel-eared squirrels cache excess pine seeds, acorns, and fungi for the winter. Instead of making a few large caches, the way red squirrels and yellow pine chipmunks do, the tassel-eared squirrel scatter-caches his food, burying just a few seeds and nuts at a time in shallow holes. Along the Santa Catalina Mountain trail, I found another typical stash—a shriveled gray-brown mushroom in the crotch of a snag. Tassel-eared squirrels also stash fungi on the dense, table-flat mats of witch's brooms.

Though it is foolish to fault a system that has seen the squirrels through thousands of years, their caches seem strangely haphazard and inadequate. They seldom cache enough to build a reliable, sufficient store for the winter and will not retrieve the caches when more than a foot of snow covers the ground. What's more, after millennia of astute observation, trial, and error, Steller's jays have become wise to this easy food source. They watch tassel-eared squirrels make their caches, then dig them up when the squirrels move away.

Even if the squirrels tried to cache large amounts of food for the winter, they would often be unable to do so because autumn crops in the ponderosa pine forest are so unreliable. Cone crops are often meager; in one of every four years, the pines produce almost no cones at all. Moreover, if monsoon rains fail to provide at least one full week during which the humus humidity is greater than 70 percent, truffles will not mature.

The tassel-eared squirrel survives these losses by feeding on the pine itself. The ground beneath ponderosa pines in the squirrel's range is usually littered with green-needled twig clippings. Year-long, but especially in lean winter months, the squirrel nips the pines' twig ends, sometimes eating their tender terminal buds, then peels off the twigs' tender cambium. Bigger even than a western gray squirrel at twelve inches long and roughly two pounds, the tassel-eared squirrel is the only large squirrel species that can subsist on bark, which is hard to digest and low in nutrients. Eating hypogeous fungi in autumn actually prepares the squirrel for a winter diet of bark, because the fungi stimulate growth of bark-digesting microbes in the squirrel's digestive tract.

When deep, uncrusted snow covers the ground, tassel-eared squirrels remain in the pines' crowns, gorging on cambium and returning to their pine-twig nests to digest. During a snowy winter, the squirrels may be confined to the trees for weeks. Their survival hinges on a good choice of nest site, which depends as much on the trees surrounding the site as on the nest tree itself. The squirrels winter best when they nest in a mature tree within a stand of yellowbellies whose bushy crowns grow close enough together for the squirrels to leap among them. These mature trees have the sweetest cambium and the most abundant seed crops, and create a safe, aerial pathway to more food.

Though the mature pine forest sustains the squirrels, it does not favor them, nurturing equally their ablest predators. From the gold-columned pines plummets a blur of gray. Preoccupied with his diggings, a tassel-eared squirrel bounds too late toward the closest trunk. The blow eviscerates him and he dies instantly. Moments later he is airborne, impaled on the needle talons of a northern goshawk.

Tilting and folding her long, rudderlike tail and elliptical wings in minute, split-second adjustments, the goshawk hurtles through the forest. In a stand of wide-bellied pines, she arcs into the canopy and folds her three-foot span of wings, dropping with her prey onto a wide nest. Three gangly chicks scramble to her, their mouths gaping in anticipation.

Goshawks are masters of the ancient forest, weaving through the maze of trunks beneath its high canopy with flawless grace. When hunting, they survey the forest from a tree perch, then dive after prey in short, powerful bursts of flight. Widely distributed but uncommon throughout most of their range, goshawks inhabit old-growth forests from Alaska to Mexico, many of these composed predominantly of ponderosa pines.

In the Southwest, they hunt mountain cottontails, blue grouse, ravens, red squirrels, northern flickers, least chipmunks, Steller's jays, and tassel-eared squirrels beneath the pine canopy. In winter, when least chipmunks hibernate and red squirrels tunnel safely beneath the snow, tassel-eared squirrels become their mainstay.

Many other animals share in the bounty of the ancient pine forest. Pileated woodpeckers, prehistoric spectacles with their fierce red helmets, black capes, and hoarse, guttural cries, wing through the ponderosa pine forests of the Northwest in sweeping arcs and excavate perfect circles that open into nest holes in the rotting heartwood of yellowbellies and snags. The great, ragged rectangular holes in these trees are theirs as well, battered out as they probe for grubs and carpenter ants.

I once thumped on a pine snag in Montana and looked up to see two northern flying squirrels peering down from an old pileated woodpecker hole. The flammulated owl, barely bigger than a robin, also nests in these holes or in other natural hollows in the old trees. Throughout most of the West, these insect-eating owls

inhabit ancient ponderosa pine forests almost exclusively. In the pine forest's grass-lined understory, they find more moth and grasshopper species than in any other western coniferous forest.

Mature pines often have broken or dead tops from lightning strikes or insect damage. With their upward growth halted, the pine crowns become dense and bushy, their trunks rotted and hollow, making ideal den sites for pine martens. Threatened Mexican spotted owls nest in Southwest old-growth stands where ponderosa pines mix with firs and spruces.

On the Kaibab Plateau north of Grand Canyon, I walked through the Jack Jolly timber sale, logged just a few months earlier. Loggers had cut hundreds of yellow pines, but had left dozens of others, as well as countless blackjack poles. A few big pines and snags bore square, plastic tags denoting them as "wildlife trees." Symmetrical imprints of a bulldozer wound serpentine through the cut, ending in wide slash piles. This sale was a selective cut, designed to lessen the ecological impact of logging.

Individually, the remaining trees retain many of the qualities required by old-growth-dependent wildlife. Collectively, they do not, for what is left is a collection of trees, not a forest. The scattered mature pines will produce abundant cones and cambium for the tassel-eared squirrel, but their crowns are widely spaced. When two or three feet of soft snow covers the ground, as it often does on the Kaibab Plateau, squirrels that nest here may starve for lack of interwoven crowns through which to forage. The isolated old pines are also now more vulnerable to lightning strikes and blowdowns than when they stood among many others.

Logging has further reduced the tassel-eared squirrel's survival chances in the Jack Jolly sale area by degrading the habitat of mycorrhizal fungi. Wherever they traveled, bulldozers and skidders scraped away the humus layer in which fungi grow. Compacted, exposed soil dries out quickly and will not support truffles. Tassel-eared squirrels may, out of necessity, nest in this logged area, but it is marginal habitat for them, in which they will be far more susceptible to climatic fluctuations and vulnerable to predators.

Northern goshawks eat dozens of different prey species, so the reduction or loss of tassel-eared squirrels, by itself, does not necessarily mean their demise. This logged land will support robins, grouse, jays, and flickers—all goshawk prey. Nevertheless, it will not support the goshawk, whose needs run far deeper than simple prey abundance. Once a selective cut opens up the forest canopy, open-canopy raptors, especially red-tailed hawks and golden eagles, compete with adult goshawks and prey upon young goshawks, and great-horned owls take over their nests.

Historically, the Kaibab Plateau has supported a greater density of goshawks than any other forest in the lower forty-eight states. In 1972, researchers estimated 130 nesting goshawk pairs in the North Kaibab ranger district. In 1988, they counted only 60 pairs. Goshawks had abandoned 90 percent of their nest sites in areas logged during those sixteen years.

In the dense stands of saplings and blackjack poles that regenerate on logged land, neither goshawk nor flammulated owl can hunt with ease. Vigorous young trees offer fewer natural cavities for nesting flammulated owls, northern flying squirrels, and song-birds than do pithy old pines. Pileated woodpeckers will not excavate nest holes in small-diameter trees.

I speak of these animals as if researchers have solved the riddles of their existence and laid them bare and known. Indeed, researchers have uncovered myriad details about members of the ponderosa pine ecosystem. But much of the essence of their lives remains undiscovered, revealing itself in fleeting glimpses to only the most patient and persistent of observers. Huge questions linger, and with every answer learned, a raft of new questions emerges. How much undisturbed land do goshawks require to nest success-fully and rear offspring? What configuration of old growth best suits the goshawk's needs, and what land features should be included? How many nesting pairs of goshawks must exist to maintain a genetically viable population, the point below which they slide irrevocably toward extinction? Is deforestation affecting the amount of interbreeding that occurs among populations of goshawks throughout their range? What about Mexican spotted owls? Flammulated owls?

Beneath a dressing of facts and figures, our ignorance of natural processes within the ancient forest is astounding. Such ignorance in and of itself is a fine and healthy thing, fodder for humility before that which is beyond our understanding, impetus for further exploration. But political and economic pressures demand immediate management decisions in the pine forests. Every western national forest now mandates that a specific portion of the forest—in Southwest ponderosa pine forests, approximately 10 percent—be managed as old growth, without scientific evidence that these quotas are even remotely adequate to protect old-growth-dependent plants and animals.

Most of the ancient ponderosa pine forests are gone. The goshawk is now listed as a sensitive species, recommended for threatened status in the southwest portion of its range, a designation already granted to the Mexican spotted owl. The old growth remaining in western forests is widely fragmented or, as in the case of the magnificent ancient pine forests of eastern Oregon, is rapidly becoming so.

These fragmented stands are islands of habitat for the species living within them, isolated from other suitable habitat by a sea of logged land. Some effects of such fragmentation are, perhaps, predictable, but few are well documented. I wander through a designated old-growth stand on the Kaibab Plateau. The stand is surrounded by logged areas, with yawning openings between uncut pines. I think of the Kaibab squirrels and their brilliant, snowy tails. The tail that is a harmless flamboyance within the cover of the ancient forest signals to raptors like a surrender flag as the squirrel crosses these cleared lands. The genetic survival skills handed down through ten thousand generations are ill-adapted to this recently transformed landscape. If the squirrels cannot bridge the logged expanses that divide them, they may not interbreed freely across the plateau. The effects of such phenomena take years to become apparent to researchers.

How much old growth is enough? How many goshawks or Mexican spotted owls? Should we set our sights on maintaining minimum, genetically viable populations, or try to reverse their steady decline since European settlement? These are not political, economic, or even ecological questions. They are, instead, pieces of the slippery, irksome moral question of how to conduct ourselves as members of the natural world.

In 1949, Aldo Leopold clearly answered this question in *A Sand County Almanac*. "A thing is right," he wrote, "when it tends to preserve the integrity, stability, and beauty of the biotic community. It is wrong when it tends otherwise." In our subjectivistic culture, such an idea is heretical because it places absolute moral standards on our interactions with the natural world. Moreover, it directly challenges our traditional approach to land-use conflicts, in which economics generally has the final say. It is an answer that demands wholesale changes in the way we inhabit the earth, a reining-in of our power to manipulate and transform the land-scape. And for that reason, it is an answer we have assiduously and successfully ignored.

9

Living Among Old Pines

FISH CREEK MURMURS TO ITSELF in a voice like rustling cottonwood leaves as it curves past Montana's biggest ponderosa pine on its way to the Clark Fork River. Water-tossed sunlight animates the old tree's trunk and ripples on the underside of its lowest branch, thirty feet overhead. Its bark is a smooth sheath of gold flakes — with none of the dark furrows of younger trees whose bark splits deep from the pressure of their own burgeoning heartwood — as if the old pine, nearly seven feet wide, had reached equanimity after four centuries of striving.

Nearby, an interpretive sign describes how many houses could be built with its wood; a low cable fence encircles its base. The old pine, once one among thousands, now stands alone, a magnificent roadside attraction set apart like the last passenger pigeon in the Cincinnati zoo. It is a relic, out of place in the clearcuts and second-growth stands that cover the rest of the Fish Creek drainage.

Describing the ponderosa pine stands in Yosemite, John Muir wrote: "The average size of full grown trees on the western slope . . . is a little less than 200 feet in height and from five to six feet in diameter, though specimens considerably larger may easily be found." He later made note of one that was over eight feet in diameter and 220 feet high. Donald Culross Peattie recorded a ponderosa pine nearly nine feet in diameter along the banks of the Deschutes River near La Pine, Oregon, and another near Mount Adams, Washington, almost as big.

I walk one afternoon in the foothills of the Flatirons near Boulder, Colorado, with a friend who has lived in the West all his life. We climb a steep trail worn deep into the grassy hillside and enter the dappled shade of ponderosa pines. "Ah," says my friend with satisfaction. "Now *there's* a big one!" He points to a pine ahead of us. It is about eighteen inches in diameter and seventy feet tall, black-barked with hints of tawny brown. I look across the hillside. The pine is unquestionably bigger than any of the ones surrounding it.

As the great yellowbellies fall, so do our expectations of the pines; we become satisfied with less without realizing what we have lost. In doing so, we surrender the knowledge and experience of what these trees, at their best, can be. The metamorphosis of bark from gray-black to honey yellow, of branches from spindly to thick and graceful, of the pine stand from tangled to clear and spacious, requires centuries of slow growth. The texture and character of the ancient pine forest are as different from those of younger stands as golden eagles from their graceless chicks.

But if my friend truly appreciates the beauty of a small pine, does it matter that he does not know that the pine species is capable of much more? I was asked recently by a man who runs a sawmill in southern Utah what I had against small trees. What is wrong, he asked while shaking the branch of a wrist-thick Engelmann spruce, with trees like this? Surely a second-growth forest, which embodies all the potential of old growth in its slender branches, is as beautiful as—not to mention infinitely more useful than—a virgin ancient forest.

I am reminded of the church I attended as a child. It was not an ornate building, but I recall its interior as weathered and mysterious. Its hard-backed pews were of smooth oak, polished by years of wool coats and restless bodies. Simple stained-glass windows interrupted its dark walls, suggesting but not quite revealing the day that unfolded beyond them. Wrought iron lanterns hung from high beams, throwing dim light on the congregation. Heavy velvet curtains, in a rich maroon, draped shadowy confessionals.

Then, in the 1970s, the church was "modernized." When the renovations were complete, the walls were creamy white, brightly illuminated by recessed lighting. Upholstered chairs replaced the pews, and clear, angular windows the stained glass. Beige, looped carpeting covered the tile floor. Accordion-pleated vinyl walls hung on metal tracks, to divide the church into smaller units as needed. The building became surpassingly comfortable and functional—and devoid of spirit and soul.

Perhaps the most inspiring human-made place of worship is Europe's Chartres Cathedral. By the twelfth century, when most of Chartres was built, Europe's primeval forests were already nearly gone. The architects and artisans of Chartres drew upon the spiritual power of those vanishing forests, mimicking their scale, complexity, and configuration. Columns rise and spread like pine boughs across a vaulted ceiling a hundred feet high. Muted light filters through the leaded latticework of stained glass like late-day sun through the lace of needles. Shadows pool in cool recesses. Low voices, like the plaintive calls of owls, drift from cloaked alcoves and dissipate in still air. Vast hallways dwarf the human figures wandering smooth stone floors.

In the cathedral's statues, carvings, and glasswork—in its great walls, columns, buttresses, piers, and pinnacles—is the lifework of thousands, the slow accumulation of years of meticulous and inspired work, embracing a history unfathomably deeper than the memory of any one man. Each of the thousands of sculptures that inhabit its archways, walls, and niches, each of the hundreds of stained-glass panels that re-create human history in the play of shadow and light, is worthy of a lifetime of contemplation. Collectively, they inspire rapture, even fear, so fully does their cumulative beauty suggest the divine.

In the ancient forest, thousands of species of plants and animals live beneath thick columns and arching boughs. Each is glorious in its own right, astonishing as part of the finely wrought masterpiece of the forest. The giant pines that sustain them mature with glacial slowness. Though widely dispersed, their wide crowns fill the canopy. In time they fall like ruined castles and dissolve, finally, into earth. The forest they create is a place of eternal life manifested in fruition, death, decay, and rebirth.

By modern standards of utility, the cathedral and the ancient forest are maddeningly impractical, inefficient, excessive, and illogical. How much easier to heat Chartres if its ceilings were half as high, if it had fewer hallways and chambers. Imagine how many other buildings could have been built from the resources—the human lives, the acres of stone, the long years—required to create the sculptures and scrolled columns and glasswork within it. Think of all the wood going to waste in the ancient forest, with nothing more than humus coming of the old trees. A dozen blackjack pines could grow in the place of a single yellowbelly. In traditional forestry jargon, these old trees are "decadent," "overmature," and "lacking in vigor," depriving the forest and foresters of the youthful trees that would grow so much more quickly and efficiently.

Even well-meaning defenders of old growth focus on the issue of the forests' utility, though in this case as reason for preserving them. Ancient forests, they argue, may harbor potential medicines and food sources to benefit humankind. They generate tourism dollars, they prevent erosion which protects fish populations which protects the fishing industry. And so on. But as long as we justify preserving ancient forests on economic and utilitarian grounds, we will lose them, for there will undoubtedly come a time when the economics of destroying the forest community outweighs its other potential economic values. Few would justify the preservation of Chartres on the grounds of its handsome tourism revenues or the potential use of its stones in future building projects. We preserve

Chartres because it is a sacred place, uplifting in an essential and inimitable way to the human spirit.

Eugene Ionesco wrote, "If one does not understand the usefulness of the useless and the uselessness of the useful, one cannot understand art. And a country where art is not understood is a country of slaves and robots." We must preserve intact and undisturbed old-growth forests precisely because they are *not* useful in utilitarian terms. For as long as humans have lived among trees, ancient forests have been a wellspring of inspiration and sanctuary, where one might escape the illusions of ego and touch the divine.

In Europe, Christian leaders recognized this powerful spirituality. They diligently hastened the destruction of Europe's venerated old groves to suppress tree worship and bring pagans into the Christian fold. By taming the forest, they could tame the human spirit. In his book, *The Green Man*, William Anderson describes an illustration in an ancient manuscript on the life of St. Amand, a seventh-century bishop. He stands beside a blind woman who holds an ax, preparing to cut down a sacred tree. From the tree's crown two heads, representing the tree's spirit, look on in horror. When the woman does the bishop's bidding and fells the tree, her sight is restored.

In transforming the wild forest into a plantation of saplings, we hold back the advance of entropy, make sense of chaos, reduce the mystery of the forest's very existence to the level of our own comprehension. In so doing we gain a sense of control, however illusory, over aging and even death itself. Godlike, we plant the trees and dictate the course of their lives. They grow and die by our timetable, insulated from as many of nature's variables as we have power to control.

By cutting the last remnants of the West's ancient ponderosa pine stands, we reduce the pine and ourselves to the safe, known, shadowless confines of mediocrity. I am not afraid of losing the ponderosa pine species—these trees number in the hundreds of millions in the West, far more than a century ago. Instead, I fear a spiritual extinction, silent and insidious, a numbing monotony as the forest's great canopy crashes around us. Though the sacred resides in all of nature, pristine or scarred, wild or cultivated, it is most readily and powerfully apparent in that part of nature that is beyond our control. For it is most often only in the presence of wildness that we are appropriately humble and conscious of our place in the natural order.

When viewed from outside, the stained-glass windows of Chartres are dark and meaningless. Only by entering the cathedral's shadowed interior and looking out toward the light can one see the exquisitely rendered stories of humanity told in each translucent mosaic. Similarly it is only by entering the shadowed interior of the ancient pine forest, by lying on the needled earth and gazing through distant, swaying crowns that one can glimpse the particular illumination that issues from unmanipulated, ageless nature. By the grace of old pines, we enter into our own history, into an understanding of our place and worth in the landscape of the American West.

Bibliography

Anderson, R. Scott. "Development of the Southwestern Ponderosa Pine Forests: What Do We Really Know?" In *Multiresource Management of Ponderosa Pine Forests*, edited by Covington, W. Wallace et al., 15–22. Gen. Tech. Rep. RM-185. 1989.

Anderson, William. *The Green Man: The Archetype of Our Oneness with the Earth.* San Francisco: Harpercollins, 1990.

Aney, William C. "The Effects of Patch Size on Bird Communities of Remnant Old-Growth Pine Stands in Western Montana." Master's thesis, University of Montana, 1984.

Arno, Stephen F. "Fire Ecology and Its Management Implications in Ponderosa Pine Forests." In *Proceedings of Symposium: Ponderosa Pine — The Species and Its Management.* Pullman, Wash., 1989.

———. Personal interview. 5 April 1989.

———. Personal communication. 12 May 1989.

Arno, Stephen F., and Ramona P. Hammerly. *Northwest Trees.* Seattle: The Mountaineers, 1977.

Badé, William F. *The Life and Letters of John Muir.* Boston: Houghton Mifflin, 1924.

Barrett, Stephen W. "Relationship of Indian-Caused Fires to the Ecology of Western Montana Forests." Master's thesis, University of Montana, 1981.

Basso, Keith H. "'Stalking with Stories': Names, Places, and Moral Narratives Among the Western Apaches." In *On Nature*, edited by Daniel Halpern, 95–116. San Francisco: North Point Press. 1986.

Betencourt, Julio L., et al., eds. *Packrat Middens: The Last 40,000 Years of Biotic Change*. Phoenix: University of Arizona Press, 1990.

Bly, Robert. *News of the Universe: Poems in Twofold Consciousness*. San Francisco: Sierra Club, 1980.

Campbell, Joseph. *The Power of Myth*. New York: Doubleday, 1988.

Cooper, Charles F. "Changes in Vegetation, Structure, and Growth of Southwestern Pine Forests Since White Settlement." *Ecological Monograph* 30 (1960): 129–64.

Crocker-Bedford, D. Coleman. "Goshawk Reproduction and Forest Management." *Wildlife Society Bulletin* 18 (1990): 262–69.

Daubenmire, Rexford. *Plant Geography*. New York: Academic Press, 1978.

DeVoto, Bernard, ed. *The Journals of Lewis and Clark*. Boston, Mass.: Riverside Press (Houghton Mifflin), 1953.

Dillon, Richard. *Meriwether Lewis*. New York: Coward-McCann, 1965.

Douglas, David. *Journals: 1823–1827*. London: W. Wesley & Son, 1914.

Duff, Duane. Vice president of manufacturing, White Pine Sash Company. Personal interview. 20 April 1989.

Emerson, Ralph Waldo. "Nature." In *Emerson's Essays*, 380–401, New York: Thomas Y. Crowell Co., 1926.

Encyclopedia of World Mythology, 1975 ed., s.v. "The mythology of plants."

Fahey, John. *The Flathead Indians*. Norman: University of Oklahoma Press, 1974.

Fischer, William C. "Safeguarding Montana's Forest Homes: Lessons from the Pattee Canyon Fire." *Western Wildlands* 4 (Summer 1977): 30–35.

Ford, Dabney. Chief archeologist, Chaco Canyon National Monument. Personal interview. 5 November 1992.

Fowells, H. A. *Silvics of Forest Trees of the United States*. USDA-Forest Service, Agr. Handbk. #271. 1965.

Frasier, Kendrick. *People of Chaco: A Canyon and Its Culture*. New York: Norton, 1986.

Ganey, Joseph L., and Russell P. Balda. "Distribution and Habitat Use of Mexican Spotted Owls in Arizona." *The Condor* 91 (1989): 355–61.

Green, George R. *The Conifers*. Vol. 1 of *Trees of North America*. Michigan: Edwards Brothers, 1933.

Greenwood, Thomas. Montana Department of Fish, Wildlife, and Parks. Telephone interview. 12 April 1989.

Gruell, George E., Wyman C. Schmidt, Stephen F. Arno, and William J. Reich. *Seventy Years of Vegetative Change in a Managed Ponderosa Pine Forest in Western Montana.* USDA-Forest Service, Gen. Tech. Rep. INT-130. 1982.

Habeck, James. *Changes in Forest Stand Structure Related to Fire History in the Pattee Canyon Drainage, Missoula, Montana.* Contract completion report, 1985. Photocopy.

———. "Old-Growth Forests in the Northern Rocky Mountains." *Natural Areas Journal* 8 (July 1988): 202–11.

———. Pattee Canyon Land Survey Records. Manuscript. 1986. Photocopy.

Hart, Jeff. *Montana—Native Plants and Early Peoples.* Helena: Montana Historical Society, 1976.

Hawthorne, Elizabeth. *A Short Study of the Primm Property and Its Potential as a Recreation Area.* Report to Montana Department of Fish and Game. June 1977. Photocopy.

Hejl, Sallie. *Old-Growth Forests in the Northern Rocky Mountains: What Is the Problem?* USDA-Forest Service. 1 March 1989. Photocopy.

Jackson, Leroy, and Adella Begay. Navajo Nation tribal members. Personal interview. 3 November 1992.

Johnson, Philip C. *Logging Railroads of the Anaconda Copper Mining Company in Montana.* University of Montana. 1979. Photocopy.

Keith, James O. "The Abert Squirrel and Its Dependence on Ponderosa Pine." *Ecology* 46 (1965): 150–63.

Kennedy, Patricia. "Habitat Characteristics of Cooper's Hawks and Northern Goshawks Nesting in New Mexico." In *Proceedings of the Southwest Raptor Symposium,* edited by R. L. Glinski, et al., 218–27. National Wildlife Federation Sci. and Tech. Series No. 12. 1988.

Linhart, Yan B., Marc A. Snyder, and Susan A. Habeck. "The Influence of Animals on Genetic Variability Within Ponderosa Pine Stands, Illustrated by the Effects of Abert's Squirrel and Porcupine." In *Multiresource Management of Ponderosa Pine Forests,* edited by Wallace Covington et al., 141–48. Gen. Tech. Rep. RM-185. 1989.

Losensky, Jack. Forest Service ecologist. Telephone interview. 17 April 1989.

Lowery, David P. *Ponderosa Pine: An American Wood.* USDA-Forest Service. FS-254. 1984.

Manning, Dick. "Expanded harvest means future shortage." *Missoulian.* 16 October, 1988, B-1.

———. "Timber liquidation was a boardroom decision." *Missoulian.* 16 October 1988, B-6.

Maser, Chris. "Life cycles of the ancient forest." *Forest Watch* 9 (March 1989).

Maser, Chris, James M. Trappe, and Ronald A. Nussbaum. "Fungal-Small Mammal Interrelationships with Emphasis on Oregon Coniferous Forests." *Ecology* 59 (1978): 799–809.

McFarland, Jeannie. *Pine Needle Raffia Basketry.* Redmond, Ore.: Midstate Printing, 1987.

Mills, Enos A. *The Story of a Thousand-Year Pine.* Fort Collins, Colo.: 1909.

Mirov, Nicholas T. *The Genus Pinus.* New York: Ronald Press, 1967.

Mirov, Nicholas T., and Jean Hasbrouck. *The Story of the Pines.* Bloomington: Indiana University, 1976.

Montana Extension Forestry Digest. 7 (July-August 1988): 4.

Muir, John. *The Yosemite.* New York: Century, 1912.

Newman, Sandra C. *Indian Basket Weaving.* Flagstaff: Northland Press, 1974.

Peattie, Donald Culross. *A Natural History of Western Trees.* Cambridge, Mass.: Riverside Press, 1953.

Pielou, E. C. *The World of Northern Evergreens.* Ithaca: Comstock Publishing, 1988.

Pyne, Stephen J. *Fire in America: A Cultural History of Wildland and Rural Fire.* Princeton, N.J.: Princeton University Press, 1982.

Reynolds, Richard T., and Brian D. Linkhart. "The Nesting Biology of Flammulated Owls in Colorado." In *Biology and Conservation of Northern Forest Owls,* edited by R. W. Nero et al., 239–54. USDA-Forest Service, Gen. Tech. Rep. RM-142. 1987.

Reynolds, Richard T., et al. *Management Recommendations for the Northern Goshawk in the Southwestern United States.* Final Draft. USDA-Forest Service. 1991.

Seeley, Charles. Forest manager, Champion International. Personal interview. 5 April 1989.

Sieminski, Joseph. Retired Anaconda and Champion International employee. Personal interview. 12 April 1989.

Silko, Leslie Marmon. *Ceremony.* New York: Penguin Books, 1977.

States, Jack S. Northern Arizona University biology professor. Personal interview. 16 October 1992.

States, Jack S., William S. Gaud, W. Sylvester Allred, and William J. Austin. "Foraging Patterns of Tassel-Eared Squirrels in Selected Ponderosa Pine Stands." In *Proceedings of the Symposium: Management of Amphibians, Reptiles, and Small Mammals in North America,* edited by R. Szaro et al., 425–31. USDA-Forest Service Gen. Tech. Rep. RM-166. 1988.

Stevenson, A. H., Lynn F. James, and Jay W. Call. "Pine-Needle (*Pinus ponderosa*)-Induced Abortion in Range Cattle." *Cornell Veterinarian* 42 (1972): 519–24.

Teale, Edwin Way. *The Wilderness World of John Muir.* Boston: Houghton Mifflin, 1954.

Thwaites, Reuben Gold, ed. *Original Journals of the Lewis and Clark Expedition.* 8 vols. New York: Dodd, Mead & Co., 1904–5.

Turney-High, Harry Holbert. "The Flathead Indians of Montana." *Memoirs of the American Anthropological Association.* No. 48. Menasha, Wisc.: American Anthropological Association, 1937.

U. S. Department of Interior. "Treaty with the Flatheads, Etc., 1855." Vol. 2, *Indian Affairs: Laws and Treaties.* 1855.

Vanderberg, Agnes. Salish elder and member of the tribal cultural committee. Personal interview. 3 December 1988.

Weisel, George F. "The Ram's Horn Tree and Other Medicine Trees of the Flathead Indians." Reprint from *The Montana Magazine of History,* July 1951.

White, Thain. "Scarred Trees in Western Montana." Flathead Lake Lookout Museum, Lakeside, Mont., No. 8.

Tad Merrick photo

About the Author

Alexandra Murphy has been an admirer of ponderosa pines since first encountering them as a naturalist at Zion National Park. When not exploring the remote outposts of their range, she writes for regional and national publications. Murphy received a bachelor's degree in biology from Cornell University and a master's degree in environmental studies from the University of Montana. She lives and works with her husband, Robert, dividing her time between the canyons of southern Utah and the mountains of Vermont.

About the Illustrator

Robert Petty received a bachelor's degree from Washington University in St. Louis and a master's degree from the University of Montana. His drawings appear in various professional journals and books. A naturalist, artist, and educator, he helped found the Montana Natural History Center, an environmental education organization. A native of Indiana (where there are no indigenous ponderosa pines whatsoever), Petty lives in Missoula, Montana, where he is the education program coordinator for The Nature Conservancy of Montana.